CHOICES *for* CHURCHES

CHOICES *for* CHURCHES

Lyle E. Schaller

Abingdon Press
Nashville

CHOICES FOR CHURCHES

Copyright © 1990 by Abingdon Press

All rights reserved.
No part of this work may be reproduced or transmitted in any form or by any
means, electronic or mechanical, including photocopying and recording, or by
any information storage or retrieval system, except as may be expressly permitted
by the 1976 Copyright Act or in writing from the publisher. Requests for
permission should be addressed in writing to Abingdon Press, 201 Eighth Avenue
South, Nashville, TN 37202.

This book is printed on acid-free paper.

Library of Congress Cataloging-in-Publication Data

Choices for churches/Lyle E. Schaller.
  p. cm.
Includes bibliographical references.
                ISBN 0-687-06694-8
  1. Pastoral theology. 2. Sociology, Christian—United States.
I. Title.
BV4011.S32 1990
250—dc20
                                              89-27337
                                                CIP

MANUFACTURED IN THE UNITED STATES OF AMERICA

To
Stanley and Dorothy Cole
and
Erma Fitzharris

Contents

Preface

Can a Christian congregation praise God by singing from a hymnal? Or should congregational singing be restricted in Sunday morning worship to the Psalms? Should a member of a lodge be permitted to become a member of a Christian church? Should the members establish their own Christian elementary schools? Or is it acceptable for Christians to send their children to public schools? May Christians partake of alcoholic beverages?

These were among the many divisive choices that faced the members of the churches founded by the European immigrants to the United States during the eighteenth and nineteenth centuries. For hundreds of midwestern congregations the most painful issue was the lodge question. The European tradition often included a strong anti-secret society attitude. Many of the Masonic lodges in Europe displayed what was widely perceived as a militant anti-Christian stance. The Roman Catholic Church forbade members to join a Masonic lodge. The United Brethren in Christ was only one of several denominations that experienced a bitter schism over the lodge issue.

In other congregations the issue that deeply divided the membership was the choice of the language to be used in corporate worship. Those who preferred English left hundreds of parishes to found a new English-language church. One of the motivations to support parochial schools was to teach the children the mother tongue. If all the children attended the English-speaking public schools, it was inevitable that English would become the language used for the corporate worship of God. For scores of immigrant churches the final decision was not perceived as a choice between the mother tongue and English, but rather between retaining as many ties as possible with a shared past and minimizing concessions to the pressures of Americanization versus the risk of "losing our young people."[1]

This book is organized around three overlapping themes. The dominant theme is every congregation, sooner or later, is confronted with what are widely perceived to be divisive choices. Frequently this results in a choosing up of sides between those who want to perpetuate yesterday and those who are ready to welcome a new and different tomorrow.

The second theme is introduced in the first chapter and referred to repeatedly in subsequent chapters. This theme rallies to one side of that divisive issue those who want to maintain a relatively simple, uncomplicated, and easy-to-understand style of congregational life built largely around one-to-one relationships and family ties. They are convinced a congregation should be conceptualized as a worshiping community composed of individuals and families. On the other side are those who accept the fact that contemporary society is far more complicated that it once was and to minister to contemporary needs it is necessary to conceptualize that parish as a community of communities.

The natural and inevitable tension between those two radically different perspectives constitutes the central theme for both the second and third chapters and reappears in chapters 4, 5, 7, and 8.

The third theme is most congregations have far more choices open to them than the members perceive to be the case. Inasmuch as the Christian faith calls both individuals and congregations to live intentional lives, it behooves every congregation to study that whole range of possibilities as it seeks to be faithful and obedient to the call of the Lord. The definition of what it means to be faithful and obedient often produces a highly divisive discussion! Does this mean being faithful to traditions coming out of the past? Or seeking to be faithful to God's will in responding to new challenges and new opportunities? That theme is most apparent in chapters 4, 5, and 6 but it also appears in every chapter.

A strong case can be made that the churches most affected by recent changes on the North American continent are old First Church downtown, the small rural church, and those congregations located in the growing regional centers of non-metropolitan communities sometimes described as the "sixty-mile city." The last two chapters focus on these three types of churches to illustrate the theme that the choices often are more numerous and more varied than many believe.

This book is addressed to several audiences including pastors, seminarians, lay leaders, and denominational staff members who work directly with congregations. The primary audience, however, consists of the members of the governing board or the program council or the long-range planning committee who are charged with the responsibility for making those choices among alternative courses of action. Their decisions will have long-term implications for that congregation.

As they seek to understand the unique nature of their own worshiping community, as they endeavor to be attentive and responsive to God's call to this particular congregation, and as they seek to exercise foresight and wisdom in making those choices, they carry a heavy burden. This book is intended, not to lighten that burden, but to provide a larger context and to offer insights that will help these leaders make informed and thoughtful choices.

Note

1. A fascinating account of how one congregation responded to a series of divisive choices is told in the history of the Third Reformed Church of Holland, Michigan, by Elton J. Bruins, *The Americanization of a Congregation* (Grand Rapids: Wm. B. Eerdmans Publishing, 1970).

CHAPTER
ONE

Community or Society?

If you have a weekly newsletter, you should plan to include at least forty different names in every issue," urged the lecturer at the annual pastor's school. "If you mail it monthly, you should try to include at least one-half of the names of your members in every issue. Remember! You want people to read it, and people like to read about themselves and their friends, neighbors, and kinfolk. Follow the model of the old county seat weekly of the 1930s. The primary reason people subscribed to it and read it was because of the names and the accounts of the daily life of that community. Births, weddings, funerals, quilting bees, barn raisings, fires, and community events constituted the important news for that community. The good editor recognized that was the fabric of daily life, and that sold papers. If you make your parish newsletter a diary of the life of your members, people will read it. You can sneak in a brief message from the pastor and a few short articles about program or finances or missions, but most of the space should be devoted to what happened with your people. Who's in the hospital? Who just returned from vacation? Who just had a baby? Who celebrated their fiftieth wedding anniversary? Who is about to change jobs? That's the news your people will be eager to read about in your parish newsletter!"

What is your reaction to this advice?

It clearly was excellent advice for the person about to launch a new weekly newspaper in small town America in 1907. It also was good advice for the pastor of a rural church in 1954. It deserves serious consideration by the person who is editing the monthly newsletter for the two-hundred-member Iowa congregation that includes a couple of dozen members who spend the winter in the Sunbelt. It is misleading advice for the editor of the weekly newsletter of the very large Protestant church today!

Back in 1887 a German sociologist, Ferdinand Tönnies, published a landmark study, *Gemeinschaft und Gesellschaft.* In this exceptionally influential book the author distinguished between two basic expressions of human relationships. The smaller *(Gemeinschaft)* is what we call community. *Gemeinschaft,* or community, is a small-scale component of the larger society. In a community people know one another intimately, they can inquire about your spouse or your children or your parents correctly by name. The members of that community (which is not always defined in geographical terms) share a common value system, and it includes a high degree of homogeneity. The family is the basic building block in creating community. This definition of community places a high value on family ties, bloodlines, habits, land, place, neighborhood, friendship, traditions, morality, virtue, respect, dignity, small voluntary associations, loyalty, cooperation, and mutual support. Those who argue that the small church is the best expression of the worshiping community can find enormous support in the writings of Tönnies. The small church in rural Iowa in 1907 often represented this version of human relationships.

The larger of these two forms of human relationships, *Gesellschaft,* represents a subsequent stage and is larger, more complex, and characterized by a greater degree of individualism, anonymity, and depersonalization of inter-personal relationships. The basic building blocks for

Gesellschaft are associations, corporations, institutions, busi-
nesses, legal obligations, economic pressures, rationality,
intentionality, individualism, and titles. A rough translation of
that term is society. The small town weekly newspaper in 1907
was a part of the glue that reinforced a sense of community.
The *New York Times,* the *Chicago Tribune,* the *Los Angeles
Times,* the *Washington Post,* and the *Wall Street Journal* are
newspapers designed to serve a larger and far more complex
society, built around institutional and competing economic
and political forces.[1] The village church on the green in New
England represented *Gemeinschaft.* That big downtown
congregation in 1955 or the huge suburban church of today
usually represents *Gesellschaft.*

The huge central city school system functions in a setting
we can call *Gesellschaft* while the one-room country school
with one teacher for eight grades benefited from a setting
called *Gemeinschaft.* One of the price tags on the
consolidation of the public schools during the middle third
of the twentieth century is that it represented a change from
Gemeinschaft to *Gesellschaft.* One reason school consolidation did not achieve all of the promised benefits, but did
produce unforeseen serious problems, was that no one
recognized this move from *Gemeinschaft* to *Gesellschaft*
had to be part of that process of consolidation.

Similarly the merger of the sixty-member church
meeting in a small white frame building along a rural road
into the seven-hundred-member congregation in a city of
thirty-five hundred residents is not simply a merger of two
churches of the same denomination. It is an attempt to
combine *Gemeinschaft* and *Gesellschaft,* to merge one
small community into a large and complicated society.

What Are the Implications?

One of the obvious implications of this conceptual
framework is that the small town congregation with a

couple of hundred members probably will be well advised to model the weekly or monthly newsletter on the small town weekly newspaper of 1907.

By contrast, the weekly newsletter of the eleven-hundred-member urban church probably should allocate far less space to what happened in the lives of the individual members and concentrate on news from the various classes, committees, boards, organizations, choirs, societies, fellowships and from the staff. While the newsletter from the small church in rural America will devote considerable space to the past, the newsletter from the large urban church should devote large quantities of space to special events, programs, and meetings yet to come. The time line of the small church's newsletter will be from last week through the next six to twelve weeks.

A second use of this conceptual framework may be for those who seek to understand what happened when the 240,000-member United Presbyterian Church in the United States of America (a *Gemeinschaft*-type religious body) united in 1958 with the 2.6 million-member Presbyterian Church in the United States (a *Gesellschaft*-type institution). Parallels can be seen in looking at the 1960 merger that produced the American Lutheran Church in America or the 1968 merger that produced The United Methodist Church or the 1988 merger that created the Evangelical Lutheran Church in America. It is not easy to retain the characteristics and values inherent in *Gemeinschaft* when that larger and more complex organization resembles *Gesellschaft*. One natural and predictable result is a sense of alienation among those who feel their *Gemeinschaft*-type organization has been replaced by *Gesellschaft*. A second is a lack of sympathy and patience from those who came from the *Gesellschaft*-type organization with those expressions of alienation.

A similar set of feelings surfaces when the small *Gemeinschaft* theological seminary that has concentrated for decades on preparing students for the pastorate merges with the larger, more complex self-identified graduate school of theology that seeks to prepare students for a growing variety of specialized ministries, for entrance into the secular labor force, as well as for service as parish pastors. When *Gesellschaft* swallows *Gemeinschaft*, the result will be more disruptive than simply a loud belch.

Another value in this conceptual framework is in understanding the feelings of those who are members of a *Gemeinschaft*-type congregation, and especially those in this type of church in the rural South and Midwest, when they respond to statements, policies, and proposals issued from the *Gesellschaft*-type national denominational headquarters.

This conceptual framework also helps explain why it is so difficult to design one continuing education event to meet the needs of people from *Gemeinschaft* congregations and also representatives from *Gesellschaft* churches. It is extremely difficult to prepare an agenda that will be meaningful and satisfying to both!

This frame of reference can be useful in producing a more sympathetic and understanding response to the feelings of the lifelong residents of the small community who are disturbed to discover that the huge influx of new residents does not simply mean a larger population. It means *Gemeinschaft* is being replaced by *Gesellschaft*. The new societal norms are undermining the old communitarian attitudes, values, and culture.

For the reader of this book this distinction between *Gemeinschaft* and *Gesellschaft* provides a useful context for looking at the choices available to churches. Many, many churches find that represents a distressing choice.

The first example of the tension produced by that choice is in the next chapter when the issue is a choice between building a sense of community that is open to all the members versus conceptualizing that congregation as a community of communities. Another is in the third chapter when the choice may be between building congregational life around a network of one-to-one relationships *(Gemeinschaft)* or around a huge, varied, and complex program *(Gesellschaft)*. A third illustration of this dichotomy often appears when the choice is between growing older together or growing younger and larger. Another is in the debate over relocation. A fifth illustration of that conflict is described in the last chapter on the church in the sixty-mile city. The parents, who place a high value on *Gemeinschaft*, continue to worship with the same congregation they have been members of for decades. Their adult children, who live only a few hundred yards away, drive ten or fifteen or twenty miles each way to be part of what appears to those parents to be a *Gesellschaft*-type church in the city. It is possible to understand why strangers would choose that church, but why would our own children do that?

Perhaps the first choice most readers of this book have to make as they help plan for the next decades of their congregation's ministry is to choose between being a *Gemeinschaft*-type worshiping community or seeking to fulfill the expectations that go with being a *Gesellschaft* church.

If sentiment alone governs that decision, in the vast majority of churches the majority of the people will pick the *Gemeinschaft* image. Therefore it may be wise to examine that choice in a larger context and seek to discover what the Lord is calling this congregation to be and to do in the years ahead.

Note

1. The origins of this chapter can be traced back to Sally Foreman Griffith, *Home Town News: William Allen White and the Emporia Gazette* (New York: Oxford University Press, 1989), to a review of that book by David M. Kennedy, "National News," *The Atlantic,* January 1989, pp. 111-15, to two parish consultations conducted in Emporia, Kansas, and to insights gained from parish consultations with other small town and rural congregations.

CHAPTER TWO

Choices in Style of Ministry

Why do we need such a large staff?" demanded the sixty-six-year-old Harold Olsen as he met with the other members of the finance committee at Trinity Church one Tuesday evening. "This is my first time back on this committee in over twenty years, and I'm amazed at the size of our payroll! My wife and I joined this congregation back in 1952 when the Reverend Harrison was the pastor. I remember the fuss that was created when we first hired a part-time director of Christian education. Up until that time Reverend Harrison did nearly everything by himself. Violet Phillips was the church secretary and also directed the choir, and Alf Johnson worked half-time as the janitor. That was our total payroll. Now we have eleven people on the payroll! I'll grant that most of them are part-time, but the congregation today isn't as large as it was in the 1950s. I checked in the office this afternoon and last year our worship attendance averaged 468 for Sunday morning compared to 516 back in 1954. We do report nearly a hundred more members than we had back in 1954, but that probably means it's time to purge the rolls again. I think the time has come to take a careful look at that payroll and see if it can be slashed. I can't believe we need that many people on the staff!"

"I know this is going to sound strange to some of you," apologized the Reverend William Barker, the beloved pastor of the 203-confirmed-member Fairlawn Church, "but I need more help." The occasion was the quarterly meeting of the pastoral relations committee with Bill Barker.

"When I came here nine years ago, we had 168 members, so I can't call this spectacular growth," continued Pastor Barker, "but the work load seems to have gone up more rapidly than the increase in membership."

"What do you need for help?" asked Mary Rice, who had chaired this committee for the past three years. "I have no problem with your request. A lot of us believe you are overworked. I teach fourth-graders in the Highland School and when my class was increased from 29 to 31 two years ago, I could tell the difference. My job was a lot harder. Here you have over 200 members plus children and constituents. Tell us what you need and we'll do the best we can to help."

"I second everything Mary has said," declared Evan Hillstrom. "In addition to being pastor, a preacher, an administrator, a teacher, and an evangelist, you're also everyone's confidant, friend, counselor, and advocate. Tell us what kind of help you believe you need, and we'll see what we can do to have it included in next year's budget."

These two incidents illustrate several changes in our society as well as the changing needs in the churches. One example is staffing. Today the typical Protestant congregation requires more staff for the same number of members than was the accepted standard forty years ago. One reason for that is the gradual disappearance of many of the forces that both complemented and reinforced parish life. These range from the increased complexity of life to the shift in the primary point of socialization (where people meet and make friends) from the neighborhood to the place of work, the place of education, the place of recreation, and the place of shopping. Other factors include the aging of the church-going population in several denominations, the growing number of mothers employed outside the home, the increased level of affluence, the demand for higher quality, the expanded expectations younger generations have of the church which has increased the range of programming, and the change in the role of denominational agencies.[1]

These two incidents also illustrate the shift in our society from generalists to specialists. Today institutions, organized around providing services to people, are expanding the role of the specialists. Examples include schools, medical clinics, social welfare agencies, hospitals, counseling services, physical fitness centers, and banks as well as the churches.

These two incidents also illustrate the differences in how congregations are organized to carry out their ministry.

The Place of Organizations

Back when the Reverend Leonard Harrison was the pastor at Trinity Church in the late 1940s and early 1950s, the ministry of that congregation was organized largely around three focal points. The most highly visible, and the one most of the people would have identified as central, was corporate worship. The Sunday morning and Sunday evening worship services were the top priorities in how Mr. Harrison scheduled his time, and many of the members evaluated him largely on his competence as a preacher.

A second focal point was the personality, gifts, skills, and talents of Mr. Harrison as a pastor. When he retired in 1958 at the conclusion of a nineteen-year pastorate, many of the old-timers mourned their loss. They had said farewell to a beloved pastor, an inspiring preacher, and a tireless leader. Many were sure that his retirement meant the beginning of the end for Trinity Church. For several score members his departure also meant saying good-bye to a close personal friend.

An overlapping part of that picture at Trinity was an impressive network of organizations that were largely owned, operated, and staffed by lay volunteers. The biggest of these was the Sunday school. On at least thirty Sundays of the year the average attendance in Sunday school exceeded the attendance at worship. For the first several years of his tenure the Reverend Leonard Harrison clearly recognized he was, at best, the second most influential leader at Trinity Church. During the 1940s the most influential leader was Stanley Owens, the Sunday school superintendent. A few weeks after celebrating his fiftieth birthday in 1932, Stanley Owens was elected to succeed his recently deceased father as Sunday school superintendent. Stanley was the logical choice. He had been the assistant superintendent for fourteen years. Even more influential, he had good bloodlines. When Stanley was killed in an automobile accident in late 1951, his death was followed by two significant changes. The first was the Reverend Harrison began to be recognized as the most widely respected and influential leader at Trinity Church.

The second was the decision to employ a part-time director of Christian education. This produced several other changes. The most obvious was the expansion of the program staff. This precedent was reinforced a few years later when Violet Phillips retired. She was succeeded by another full-time church secretary, but a different person was hired on a part-time basis to direct the choir and to expand the ministry of music.

From the Reverend Leonard Harrison's perspective three big changes occurred. The one that took some time to get accustomed to was the change from being simply the pastor to being head of the program staff. The one he enjoyed the most was the increase in his authority. For many years a standing joke at Trinity Church was that when Stanley Owens' father died, that had changed the lines of accountability. Up until that point Stanley, as both a son and as the *assistant* superintendent of the Sunday school, clearly was accountable to the senior Mr. Owens. Stanley's leadership style led many to conclude he now was accountable only to God. A few claimed Stanley believed the reverse was true.

It was absolutely clear to everyone, however, that the Sunday school superintendent was *not* accountable to the pastor. Following Stanley's death and given (a) the rubber stamp role of the Christian education committee (for many years it had been the Sunday school board) under Stanley's leadership, (b) the lengthening tenure of the Reverend Leonard Harrison, (c) the personality and leadership style of Mr. Harrison, and (d) the employment of a laywoman as the part-time director of Christian education, no one challenged the fact that both she and Mr. Harrison saw her as accountable to the pastor.

Today Trinity Church has a full-time ordained person as the minister of education, and the Sunday school attendance is slightly less than one-half what it was in 1950, Stanley Owens' last full year as superintendent.

In the eyes of many, the best organized and the strongest of all the organizations at Trinity Church in the early 1950s was the women's fellowship. It included more than three-hundred active women, raised large sums of money for missions, sponsored two dinners and a bazaar every year, and provided the money to furnish the new kitchen when Trinity Church undertook the construction of a large addition in 1954. The women's fellowship was divided into twelve circles—each averaging 18 to 30 in attendance at their meetings. The monthly general meetings usually attracted 120 to 160 women.

Today the women's fellowship is down to five circles, the monthly general meetings attract 35 to 40 women, and the total membership is reported to be 118, but that includes at least two dozen shut-ins. Those dinners to raise money for missions were abandoned in the early 1970s when it became impossible to enlist the necessary volunteers. The annual bazaar was dropped three years ago for similar reasons. As one women said, "I would rather give an extra $20 and not have to do all that work. I'm too old for that." One way to tell when you are old is when your financial reserves exceed your energy reserves.

The organizational life of Trinity Church in the 1950s also included a large men's fellowship that met eleven times a year on the second Tuesday evening of the month. Their annual schedule included the February sweetheart's dinner to which the wives were invited, a weekend retreat at the denominational camp every September which was both a mountaintop spiritual experience for many of the men and also a means of assimilating new members into the group, a pancake breakfast every October to raise money for their mission project, and one or two major work projects at the church. In the 1954–55 church year, for example, the men's fellowship contributed a combined total of 3,200 hours of volunteer labor in construction of that addition to the building.

A fourth strong organization was the high school youth group. A fifth was the 43-voice chancel choir. A sixth was the athletic program, which included a men's softball team and two (one for 17-25 year-olds and one for men age 26 and over) basketball teams.

Although it was the smallest, in terms of numbers, one of the most closely knit organizations at Trinity Church in the 1950s was a group of a dozen young families, "The Weekenders," who went on weekend family camping trips together five or six times every year. Two couples, both in their late twenties, were the organizers, cheerleaders, recruiters, recreation leaders, Bible study teachers, and publicity agents for this venture. Harold Olsen and his wife, Lillian, met and made several score friends when they went camping with this group shortly after joining Trinity Church in 1952. Today Harold and Lillian still go "camping," but it is in their Airstream mobile home, and none of their fellow campers are from Trinity Church. One of the highlights of "The Weekenders' " experience was when the Reverend and Mrs. Leonard Harrison accompanied them for a weekend. This happened only once. One reason they went was that the Harrisons' son, Jack, a second-year seminarian, was scheduled to be the guest preacher that weekend. His parents concluded he would be more comfortable, since this was his first time in that pulpit, if they had an excuse to be out of town, so they invited themselves to go camping with "The Weekenders."

These seven organizations shared several important characteristics.

1. Each was lay-led. They were not dependent on paid program staff members either for their origin or for their continued existence.

2. Each generated its own leadership out of the group.

3. Each represented a "small church" or a homogeneous unit, within that larger and somewhat anonymous collection of people called Trinity Church. Each organization provided easy opportunities for people to meet and make new friends. The adult Sunday school classes, "The Weekenders," the chancel choir, the circles in the women's fellowship, and the athletic teams were specially strong examples of this.

4. Each one was an attractive entry point for newcomers and made valuable contributions in the assimilation of new members.

5. None of them required much of the pastor's time and energy. The Reverend Harrison tried to attend at least two-thirds of the meetings of the men's fellowship, but he never attended choir rehearsal, rarely met with the women's fellowship (unless it was over a meal), never participated in any of the athletic events, even as a spectator, and he rarely taught a Sunday school class. He did spend many hours recruiting and working with adults who constituted the volunteer leadership for the youth group. For several months between Stanley Owens' death

and the arrival of the part-time director of Christian education, he was heavily involved with Sunday school, but that was only temporary.

6. Four of the seven benefited greatly from the time and talents of Mrs. Harrison. Year after year she taught in the children's division of the Sunday school, twice she finished out a term as president of the women's fellowship in addition to her two full terms, she served as the substitute organist for eleven years, and for five years she was a volunteer counselor with the high school group.

7. Every one of the seven benefited from the existence of a strong denominational support system. In this case it was the regional judicatory that (a) owned and operated the camp where "The Weekenders" went three or four times a year, (b) planned and administered those mountaintop spiritual weekend retreats for the men, (c) provided a range of resources including summer camping experiences, quarterly regional rallies, and annual work camp-mission trips to reinforce the youth program as well as offering training events for volunteer counselors, (d) offered twice-a-year workshops for choir directors, and (e) scheduled annual regional tournaments for church-sponsored basketball and softball teams. Many of these were planned and administered by committees of volunteers under the umbrella of that regional judicatory.

8. Both the regional judicatory and the national agencies of the denomination provided a range of resources to support the Sunday school and the women's fellowship including study materials, rallies, leadership training events, teacher training workshops, challenges to set and exceed goals, visiting speakers, and limited on-site consultations.

9. Each one of these seven organizations was built in part around a distinctive and growing sense of caring for one another. With some of the adult Sunday school classes and circles in the women's fellowship, this eventually became the number one unofficial reason for their continued

existence. These became redemptive religious communities where a member was loved, cared for in time of trouble, forgiven for sins of omission and commission, affirmed and accorded the respect that goes with being one of God's unique creations. The more pronounced this evolution into mutual support groups, the greater the likelihood these also became exclusionary classes and circles that made newcomers feel like trespassers.

10. While it was rarely mentioned, each of these seven organizations was heavily dependent on networks of existing kinship and friendship ties when it came to enlisting both leaders and workers. A common reason for accepting a request to help was, "Okay, I guess I owe you one."

11. Together these seven organizations provided a sense of continuity following the retirement of the Reverend Leonard Harrison in 1958. Several of his strongest supporters and biggest boosters were absolutely sure Trinity Church would be confronted with a crisis when he left. A few of them got together and persuaded him to postpone his retirement an extra year because of their fears. When he did retire, Mr. Harrison was followed by an introverted, thirty-year-old minister who turned out to be a complete mismatch and left after two troubled years. While many of the members decreased their frequency of attendance at worship during this period, and the Sunday evening attendance dropped so low the new minister canceled it, these seven organizations maintained nearly all their strength and continued to provide a sense of belonging, cohesion, unity, and meaning for hundreds of the members.

Trinity Church in the 1950s represented one approach to organizing a congregation. It was organized largely, but not completely, as a federation of lay-led, self-governing, largely self-financing, and self-propagating organizations. This once was a widely followed approach to building a congregation. It is still used today. It is less common today in Presbyterian or

Methodist or Christian Church (Disciples of Christ) or United Church of Christ or American Baptist circles than it was in the 1950s. It remains a widely followed organizing principle in black churches, in the Southern Baptist Convention, and in scores of relatively new, large, and rapidly growing nondenominational churches.

Another, and somewhat different, example of building around the strength and internal cohesion of an organization can be seen in scores of Lutheran congregations in which the Christian day school provides a sense of distinctive purpose, serves as an entry point for newcomers and is governed by a powerful board composed of lay volunteers.

Back in the 1950s both the Methodist Church and the Christian Church (Disciples of Christ) used this concept of a strong organizational life as a means of building large congregations with a comparatively small program staff. During subsequent decades both of these denominations (a) experienced substantial numerical declines in membership, (b) saw the organizational life wither in hundreds of churches, and (c) reported a decline in the number of large congregations during those years when the total number of very large Protestant churches in the United States more than tripled.

Although it would be an oversimplification of the facts to offer a single factor analysis, the decline in the organizational life and the shrinkage in the number of large churches appear to be more than a coincidence. In Ohio, for example, the predecessors of what became The United Methodist Church reported a combined total of seventeen congregations that averaged eight hundred or more at worship in 1965. Twelve of the seventeen also reported an average attendance in Sunday school of five hundred or more. Twenty-one years later only five of those seventeen reported an average worship attendance of six hundred or more, and only one reported an average attendance in Sunday school of five hundred or more. For all of the churches from that denomination in Ohio, the average attendance in Sunday school plunged from a combined total of 296,400 in 1965 to less than 117,000 in 1987—and worship attendance dropped by 30 percent.

A similar pattern prevailed in Iowa. In 1965 two dozen Methodist congregations averaged five hundred or more at worship with a combined average attendance of over 16,000. By 1986 the combined average worship attendance of these twenty-four churches had dropped to 11,000 and only seven still averaged over five hundred at worship. The combined average attendance in Sunday school for these two dozen Methodist churches plunged from 11,500 in 1965 to 5,300 in 1987. In California Methodism the number of congregations averaging five hundred or more at worship dropped from 62 in 1965 to 15 in 1986, average attendance in Sunday school declined from 115,000 in 1965 to 40,000 twenty-one years later, and membership fell by 30 percent, while the population of the Golden State grew from 17.5 million in 1965 to 27 million in 1986. Strong organizations can be powerful cohesive forces as well as provide attractive entry points for newcomers.

Lest anyone be misled by this description of one approach to organizing congregational life, this is far from the perfect system. It does encourage lay participation and can give individual lay leaders a sense of power and control. Strong organizations do provide continuity. This approach can create extremely attractive and open entry points for newcomers (especially the ministry of music and athletic programs). It can be a low cost and highly effective means of assimilating many of the new members and enabling them to quickly gain a feeling of belonging. It usually is a thrifty approach since it requires comparatively few paid staff. It does offer people a choice from among several attractive points of involvement.

The Limitations Should Not Be Ignored!

On the other hand, this approach to ministry requires an exceptionally secure pastor, both personally and professionally, who is not threatened by this diffusion of power. This approach can result in remarkably attractive and powerful organizations that suggest the tail is wagging the dog and that Word and Sacrament are of secondary importance and value in that worshiping community. This approach often creates conflicts in setting priorities, in scheduling, in the use of space, and in the competition for the loyalty of valued lay volunteers. It can create competitive cliques. In too many churches it has produced one organization that has been diverted from its original purpose into becoming a powerful and persistent lobby seeking the resignation or early retirement of the pastor. It is easy for these organizations to become self-centered, inward-oriented, and exclusionary as the members find it comfortable to grow old together. In at least a few churches one of the price tags carried a dollar sign. Members of these attractive organizations felt the first claim on their financial contributions to that church was held by a favorite organization. The congregational budget was a second priority. This also often meant that the total congregational support for benevolences and missions was understated by several thousands of dollars because the money that went through the organizational treasuries never was reported as part of the total financial base of that parish. Although not the most pressing problem in the world, this does trouble some people.

For congregations averaging fewer than five hundred to seven hundred at worship, this approach to ministry also requires a strong supportive system from denominational agencies with a continuing congregational orientation. If and when the staff and/or boards of denominational agencies place a higher priority on issue-centered ministries, this may require resources that otherwise could be used to strengthen the organizational life of congregations. If these are widely perceived as highly divisive issues, this may undercut the organizational life of congregations.

By contrast, the very large congregations typically do not

require a strong denominational support system. They provide their own. They schedule their own retreats, often at a retreat center owned by that congregation. They can afford the specialized personnel required to staff lay leadership training events, to write and publish study materials, and to create new ministries. They can arrange their own mission-work camp trips and enlist and support their own missionaries. These large churches do not need the denominational structure or resource system, which is one reason they are perceived as a threat by those who are convinced denominational loyalty requires a widespread sense of dependency.

Another price tag on building a congregation around an interlocking network of lay-led organizations can be illustrated by the responses to the question asked of members, "What does your minister do best?" The ideal response is, "Preaching!" A second best answer may be, "While our minister is not an outstanding pulpiteer, we do benefit from a carefully designed worship experience every week that is enriched by the prayers, the anthem, the hymns, and the fact that we know our pastor loves every one of us. That is reflected in every part of our worship together from the greeting and announcements to the prayers to the benediction."

If the sermon is dull, incomprehensible, designed to evoke feelings of guilt among the listeners, too long, poorly organized, boring, filled with expressions of self-pity for the preacher, or without any redeeming religious value, a significant number of members, who find their sense of belonging fulfilled in one of these organizations, such as the adult Sunday school, often find it easy to "skip church today."

Although not as common in the North and in the old-line Protestant denominations as it was thirty years ago, the power of the organizational life is still one approach to ministry favored by thousands of churches in the South, in

California, and in the Southwest. It also often is the approach followed by large nondenominational churches today in both the United States and Canada.

When it is abandoned, it often produces the negative comments voiced by Harold Olsen in the opening pages of this chapter as costs do go up and the numbers frequently do go down.

The Appeal of One-to-One Relationships

The most widely used approach to ministry, however, and the most popular with many of the clergy as well as with a large number of lay leaders is the one illustrated earlier by the Reverend William Barker's request for more help and the sympathetic and positive response his plea evoked. This is to organize the parish around an inclusive network of one-to-one relationships with the pastor at the center of that network.[2]

The extroverted, loving, gregarious, outgoing, smiling, caring, genial, affable, friendly, and approachable pastor represents the ideal minister in the minds of many members. It is not unusual for several dozen members to be able to assert confidently and proudly, "I'm one of the four or five closest friends our minister has in this entire congregation."

This, of course, is a more difficult role for the minister who is introverted, who appears to be less approachable, who prefers things and ideas to people, who enjoys being alone, or who stays for only two or three years before seeking to move on to greener pastures.

While it may not represent an intentional strategy, thousands of small congregations are organized largely around worship, the Sunday school, the women's organization, and that network of one-to-one relationships. Many of these one-to-one relationships are pastor-parishioner while others are parishioner-parishioner relationships. Frequently these also are reinforced by kinship ties and/or a common ethnic or nationality background. One of the attractions that brings people together on Sunday morning is the corporate worship of God. Another is the chance to be with close friends they haven't seen for three or four or five days.

Occasionally one will encounter a congregation of 700 to 3,500 confirmed members built largely on one-to-one relationships with the pastor or the senior minister at the hub of that network, but that represents less than 1 percent of all the very large Protestant congregations in the nation. This usually requires a rare combination of gifts and skills in every staff member that include meaningful sermons, a high level of competence in communication skills, exceptionally productive work habits, and the ability to focus one's attention so intensely on each individual for several seconds that he or she leaves feeling they have enjoyed a half-hour private counseling session. Choosing one-to-one relationships as the key foundation stone for the life of the parish is most common among congregations with fewer than 200 members. Only a very tiny proportion of pastors are able to use that approach effectively with congregations including more than a couple of hundred members. Well over one-half of all Protestant congregations in the United States report fewer than 200 members and these churches account for approximately one-fifth of all Protestant church members in the nation. These are the churches in which this approach to ministry is both attractive and most common.

This approach is consistent with the concept of the pastor as the shepherd (John 10:1-18). Once upon a time this was taught in many theological seminaries as the appropriate leadership role for a minister, and it still has many advocates. The advantages are obvious for pastoral care, for preparing sermons that speak to the contemporary needs of that flock, and for winning the support of the members. The vast majority of the laity are delighted with any approach that will create a close personal relationship between them and their pastor. Young children and their parents love this ministerial style. The advantages are many.

In those parishes where this is the central organizing principle and members are asked, "What does your pastor do best?" the answers usually lift up these shepherding skills. "Our pastor excels in one-to-one relationships." "Our minister knows, loves, and cares for every one of us." "Our pastor is never too busy to give you as much time as you need." "My minister represents the father I never had, but the one I've always dreamed about." "Our pastor may not be an outstanding preacher, but he communicates God's love by his actions far more impressively than most preachers do by their great sermons."

The big liabilities of this approach have forced many denominational leaders to challenge it.

From an economic point of view it has priced many smaller churches out of the ministerial marketplace. The rapidly rising compensation for a full-time, resident, seminary-trained, and experienced pastor, especially the cost of health insurance, housing, pensions, travel allowance, and continuing education, have removed this alternative from the list of possibilities for at least 40 percent of all Protestant churches. They simply cannot afford a compensation package that comes to well over $30,000 annually, including housing, in 1990 dollars.[3]

The second limitation on this strongly relational approach is it works most effectively if the pastor is an extroverted, gregarious, emotionally secure, psychologically well-adjusted, outgoing, person-centered individual. Fewer than one-half of contemporary seminary graduates fit that description.

Third, it is most appealing in congregations in which most of the members have passed their fiftieth birthday. It is far less effective in reaching younger adults. One result is it has less appeal in those churches in which the leaders want to reach and incorporate into that fellowship more younger adults.

Fourth, it is expensive in terms of the ratio of staff per

one hundred members. Most of the clergy are limited to 168 hours a week. Building and maintaining a network of relationships with two hundred people requires a lot of time. This usually means the congregation following this approach will experience gradual numerical decline unless additional program staff are added to the payroll. That was the heart of Pastor Bill Barker's request for help.

Fifth, an effective implementation of this approach normally requires a personal and religious pilgrimage of every member over a period of a decade or two or three. It has limited effectiveness if the typical pastorate is seen as three or four or five years.

Sixth, it often produces an unhappy experience for the successor who may be perceived as a combination trespasser, intruder, alien, stepparent, foreigner, and perhaps even enemy. This predictable phenomenon can be alleviated through the use of an intentional interim minister following the end of a long-term, heavily relational pastorate, but the costs should not be ignored.

Seventh, most of the ministers who are exceptionally effective in creating and nurturing this network of one-to-one relationships have neither the time nor the inclination either to strengthen the organizational life or to expand the total program of that parish. This accentuates the natural limitations of this approach in reaching a new generation of younger members. (See chapter 5.)

Eighth, this style of ministerial leadership has been subject to considerable criticism in recent years on the grounds that it legitimatizes an authoritarian, "father-knows-best," male chauvinist and domineering role for the pastor while depicting the parishioners as mean, ornery, and inconsiderate subjects.

Finally, and perhaps the most subtle problem with this approach to ministry, is that it appears to be deceptively simple. The effective implementation of this approach demands more than simply the twenty-four-hour availability of a personable pastor. It also requires a comparatively high level of competence in counseling skills, an unselfish and powerful neighbor-centered love, an uninhibited willingness to sacrifice for others (John 10:11), a powerful evangelistic zeal (John 10:16), the ability to hear the unarticulated needs of the people, an exceptional ability to be a productive manager of one's own time while still being available to others, and a willingness to work long hours. It is a far more demanding role than it appears to be on the surface. This can be seen by studying the schedule, the gifts, the accomplishments, and the performance of that rare shepherd who cares for a flock of several hundred parishioners, that is both growing in numbers and is well fed spiritually.

Those who seek a larger context for understanding the tension between these first two approaches to ministry may find it in the first chapter. Those who prefer the world of human relationships summarized by *Gemeinschaft* will come out on the side of building parish life around that network of one-to-one relationships. The organizational approach (and the programmatic approach described later in this chapter) will have greater appeal to those who are comfortable with the *Gesellschaft* view of human relationships.

The Rarest Approach

At the other end of the spectrum in terms of frequency is what is the rarest approach to the parish ministry. This is to organize the congregation around the support of and involvement in world-wide missions.

One congregation in Pennsylvania allocates 70 to 80 percent of every dollar dropped in the offering plate to missions. It supports in whole or in part over three hundred missionaries, most of whom received the call to missionary service after uniting with that congregation. This church, which averages nearly seven hundred at worship on Sunday morning and well over five hundred on Sunday evening, has sponsored or helped in the sponsoring of literally hundreds of new missions all over this planet. It organizes and hosts an annual missionary conference that attracts several hundred participants from a score of countries every summer.

While it is relatively rare, this approach to ministry has many advantages. It provides a single unifying and highly visible organizing principle that is easy to prooftext. This highly visible focus sorts out prospective new members so only those who agree missions should be the top priority of congregational life decide to join. This reduces the possibility of diversionary conflicts over purpose and priorities. This focus is highly compatible with creating a high expectation church in which much is expected of every member. It is easy to enlist volunteers for a huge variety of responsibilities since the giving of one's time and gifts to help others is the central ethic of congregational life. The entire life of the worshiping community is based on the assumption God has given to each of His children special gifts that can be used in the building of His kingdom.

Critics often argue this excessive emphasis on missions distorts the Christian message of love, undercuts the centrality of Word and Sacrament, fosters colonialism, neglects or intimidates those members who may have deep and complex personal needs, and ignores the divine call to change the structures of society.[4] These and similar criticisms, however, rarely deter those who are persuaded that missions should be the central theme of congregational life.

These mission-centered churches emerge from a variety of sources. The most common, of course, is those Christians who take Matthew 28:18-20 literally. During the first several decades of its existence, the Augustana Lutheran Church was a mission-centered denomination. The Moravian Church in America, the Conservative

Baptist Association, and the Missionary Church are three contemporary examples of missions-centered religious bodies. Between 1870 and 1939 both the Methodist Episcopal Church and the Methodist Episcopal Church, South, were heavily oriented toward missions. An outstanding example of a mission-centered regional judicatory is the Baptist General Conference of Texas. A significant number of the relatively new nondenominational or "independent" churches of today are clearly mission-centered congregations.

Scores of mission-centered congregations trace their origins back to the day when a group of members left the church in which they were members because of the low priority given to missions and went out to found a new congregation that would give missions what they were convinced was the proper importance. Many of the "independent" or nondenominational churches founded since 1950 place an exceptionally high priority on missions and some are overwhelmingly mission-centered parishes. A significant portion of the new members attracted by these churches come in part because the denomination in which they had been reared no longer displays a strong missions orientation or because the pastor suggested missionary endeavors had become an obsolete activity for the churches. It is difficult to overstate the role of missions as an influential factor in those religious bodies experiencing substantial numerical growth.

The Family Tree

When the United States was a predominantly rural society and churches were much smaller than they are today, it was not uncommon for Protestant churches to be composed largely of people from four categories: (1) those who were related by blood to the central family tree,

(2) those members, many of whom felt themselves to be second-class citizens, who married into that family tree, (3) a few "outsiders" who were not related to that family but regularly displayed their respect and deference to that influential family, and (4) several members who carried their own credentials with them and did not require that set of kinship ties to gain respect, deference, and authority. This fourth group might include the local banker, a physician, the principal of the local high school, the number-one property owner in the community, a wealthy farmer, one or two merchants, and possibly even the minister.

Most of the potential members of this fourth category, however, usually chose to be in the most prestigious church in town and tended to avoid the congregations built around a single family tree.

The Immigrant Parish

Another approach to congregational life, which flourished in the 1840–1925 era and again since 1960, is the immigrant church. In most of these all the members, usually including the pastor, came to North America from the same land. (Incidentally, in proportion to population, Canada has had a longer, a larger, and a more varied experience with immigrant churches since 1945 than has the United States. British Columbia and Ontario offer scores of examples of vigorous, vibrant, and vital immigrant churches.)

For the two decades following America's entrance into World War II, it was not uncommon to find a variation of this theme in northern industrial communities. Near Lorain, Ohio, in 1963, for example, one congregation was composed entirely of members who had been born and reared in the same rural county in Tennessee. That common point of origin included the bivocational preacher.

A contemporary variation on this theme is the Sunbelt congregation composed largely of retirees from Pennsylvania or Iowa or Minnesota or New York or Michigan who recreate their "back home" religious subculture in a warm setting, often with the assistance of a pastor from "back home."

More visible are the Korean or Cantonese or Vietnamese or Cuban or Columbian or Puerto Rican or Mexican-American congregations.

The big disadvantage of this approach is the "next generation" phenomenon. The children of those charter members often display little interest in perpetuating the past as they grow into adulthood.

The Small Group Approach

While it no longer enjoys the popularity it did in the 1960s and 1970s, the goal of conceptualizing a congregation as a network of small face-to-face groups still has widespread appeal. It also is impossible to overstate the benefits millions of Christians have derived from being part of a loving and redemptive Bible study and/or prayer group that gave the participants the opportunity to share in one another's spiritual journey and to carry one another's burden. For many people this has turned out to be a life-changing experience as well as a chance to witness to and deepen one's own faith.

It also is impossible to overstate the value of the small group approach in reaching and ministering to a small slice of the population born after 1945. This slice includes many of those who were reared outside the Christian Church, the recently divorced, those who see themselves on a religious pilgrimage that does not include a specific and clearly defined destination, the pilgrims who were "burned out" through excessive involvement in a traditional congregational setting, and many self-identified charismatic Christians.

The limitations of this approach have kept it from becoming the universal strategy for congregational life in the United States. These limitations include: (1) a high level of competence and self-confidence is required of the minister who wants to build on the power of the small group movement—it is far easier to concentrate on building one-to-one relationships, (2) it is difficult to enlist more than 40 percent of the adult membership of a congregation in this approach unless participation in a small group is made a requirement for membership—it is far easier to organize a new congregation around the small group approach than it is to install the concept in a long-established parish, (3) some people find their religious pilgrimage is enriched by participation in a small sharing group, but eventually that pilgrimage may lead them out of that group, (4) there is a natural tendency in most intimate small groups to become exclusionary, (5) non-participants sometimes perceive these as elitist groups, (6) unless the staff includes exceptionally productive members, the small group approach usually requires a higher paid staff-to-membership ratio than most congregations believe they can afford, and (7) a change in pastors can be highly disruptive in a congregation built on the small group approach.

Although a few very large congregations have been built on the combination of (a) exceptional preaching, (b) a strong ministry of music, and (c) a huge network of small face-to-face groups, most North American congregations that find this to be a productive approach to congregational life are in the 150- to 700-member bracket.

The Power of Program

Nine basic generalizations and trends provide the context for examining a seventh approach to parish life.

The first is the larger the size, the more important a diversified and high quality program both in responding to the needs of today's members and in attracting the people who will constitute tomorrow's congregation. Second, the younger the members, the less influential are the kinship ties and one-to-one relationships and the more powerful is the program that is designed to respond to the *religious* needs of people. Third, specialization and the identification of narrowly and precisely defined audiences is crucial. A simple example is the adult Sunday school which may need to serve several sharply different audiences.[5] Fourth, the past four decades have brought the emergence of hundreds of relatively new congregations that average five hundred or more at Sunday morning worship.

Another significant recent development has been the revitalization of many long-established churches that peaked in size in the 1950s or earlier, went through a long period of numerical decline, but now are larger and stronger than ever before in their history. A sixth is that for generations the initial contact with a congregation by a prospective new member usually was on Sunday morning. Today, by contrast, many larger and numerically growing congregations report that a majority of their new members experienced their first contact with that congregation at some time other than Sunday morning. A seventh is the thoughtful and creative responses by many churches to the differences among people and the demand by younger generations for choices. An eighth is the numerical decline of several of the old-line Protestant denominations that no longer are able to sustain organizational vitality as the basis approach to congregational life. A ninth is the rapidly growing proportion of churchgoers, especially those born after 1940, who choose a large congregation in preference to a smaller one that may be meeting in a building closer to their place of residence. For many, that choice also represents a move away from the denominational family of their parents.

What do these nine generalizations have in common? One answer is program. Instead of being organized around one-to-one relationships or small face-to-face groups, a growing number of churches, and especially larger congregations, have decided to make an extensive, varied, and attractive program their central organizing theme. This may include three or four or five or six worship services every weekend, an extensive and highly redundant teaching ministry offering people a broad range of choices, an exceptionally varied ministry of music, a huge package of ministries with families that include younger children, a couple of dozen different events, classes, programs, activities, learning experiences, and services offered every week between Monday morning and Saturday evening as well as a carefully planned emphasis on a score or more of large group events every year that bring together at least a couple of hundred people for three hours or longer.

Obviously a crucial element in building program is a program staff of highly skilled, creative, energetic, and productive specialists who know how to respond to a broad range of religious and personal needs with a series of redundant and mutually reinforcing components in that huge package of program. This often is reinforced by a modest emphasis on one-to-one relationships and by organizing a large number of middle-sized groups, classes, choirs, circles, and task forces that include between a dozen and forty members.

Those who are contemplating this as the primary approach to congregational life should understand it also has its potential problems and pitfalls. The first, as already mentioned, is it requires an excellent staff. Unlike the focus on building a strong lay-led organizational life described in the first section of this chapter, the programmatic approach requires more staff, a much higher level of professional competence, better facilities, and a far larger budget. As Trinity Church switched from that dependence on lay-led organizations during Reverend Harrison's tenure to a greater emphasis on program, that created a predictable demand (a) for more staff and a larger payroll and (b) for greater economy and a smaller payroll by long-time members such as Harold Olsen who remembered very favorably those thrifty days with that network of lay-led organizations.

Second, those people who are looking for a simpler approach to congregational life may be repelled by the complexity, the pace, the choices, the competition for people's time and energy, and the seemingly minor place reserved for Word and Sacrament. Third, while much of the sense of continuity is in that program, and that requires long tenure for the staff, this approach also requires an innovative stance to respond effectively to the religious needs of new generations of members. Fourth, this approach requires an immense amount of time, energy, hard work, dedication, creativity, and energy from volunteers. This usually means either (a) problems in enlisting volunteers or (b) a highly sophisticated system for identifying, enlisting, training, placing, and supporting that network of volunteers. The magnitude of this responsibility is reflected by the fact that dozens of program-centered congregations report (a) five or six hundred different individuals accept one or more major volunteer roles every year and (b) 15 to 30 percent of them will have to be replaced annually. Finally, this approach demands a senior minister with far above average competence in building, supporting, enabling, trusting, and encouraging a large program staff, several of whom may exhibit the temperament of a prima donna. If the senior minister is a prima donna, that may use up all the space available for that role on the staff.

Word, Sacrament, and Confessions

An eighth approach to organizing the life and ministry of a parish appears to be less common than it was in the first seven decades of the twentieth century, but it is still easy to find churches organized around three highly visible and clearly defined focuses. One is the preaching of the Word, a second (which sometimes is first in the mind of the minister) is the proper administration of the Sacraments of Holy Communion and Baptism, and the third is faithful adherence to the confessional stance of that congregation, which often is stated in the constitution.

While rarely identified this clearly, in most cases a fourth ingredient to that formula is a long-tenured pastor who is convinced those are the three critical components of parish life. The contributions of this long-tenured pastor often are recognized most affirmatively many years later by the church historian who describes what happened when that pastor was succeeded by two or three short-tenured mismatches between pastor and parish.

In scores of congregations these three (or four) central organizing principles are reinforced by the operation of a Christian day school. The Christian Reformed Church, the former American Lutheran Church, the Lutheran Church-Missouri Synod, the Seventh Day Adventists, and dozens of very large nondenominational churches illustrate this approach to ministry. It also can be found, usually without the school, in some Presbyterian, Anglican, Baptist, and Reformed churches today.

The Teaching Church

One of the easiest-to-describe approaches to congregational life is represented in those parishes in which the teaching ministry is at the heart of every facet of congregational life. Every sermon is designed to help the listener comprehend a particular passage of Scripture. The choir directors accept and fulfill an instructional role. The average attendance in Sunday school approaches or exceeds the worship attendance. On any given Sunday at least two ministers are teaching in the Sunday church school, and Bible classes are offered during the week. The central organizing principle of the women's organization is learning. The ministry with youth is largely a teaching ministry—and that often means more than one-half of all participants come from nonmember families. A tremendous amount of effort is devoted to transmitting to children and youth the essentials of the Christian faith and also helping them learn and master the skills of pro-social conduct and moral behavior. A large amount of energy is spent on lay training programs to enable volunteers to improve their competence, deepen their faith, enhance their self-confidence, and motivate them to help others.

Among the more common characteristics of these churches are (1) an acceptance of the need for excellence if this approach is to be effective, (2) a large staff, most of whom came to that staff after years as a volunteer in that parish, (3) few or no denominational ties, (4) a long-tenured senior minister who introduced, inculcated, and nurtured this approach to ministry, (5) large numbers of new members who are rearing children and see this church as their number-one resource in that responsibility as well as a place to help them on their own faith journey, and (6) many visitors from other churches who come to study and learn from this teaching church.

Three Other Approaches

Anyone who reads congregational histories or who studies the very large churches of today will recognize another approach to ministry. This is to build the church around the personality of a particular minister. This was very common in

American Methodism, especially during the first half of the twentieth century, in many immigrant churches, in hundreds of Baptist churches, and in a substantial portion of the large independent churches in their early years.

The obvious liability of this approach can be seen when that magnetic central figure dies, retires, resigns, runs off with a member of the choir, or renounces the faith by word or deed.

Another approach that emerged during the 1960s was for that church to replace a ministry with members with a landlord role in which the building was used to house a variety of community organizations, their offices, and/or their programs. This was defended as a continuation of a "Christian presence" in that neighborhood and often had the advantages of eliminating the time-consuming demands of the members. Too often, however, that adversary relationship, which is a normal and predictable aspect of the landlord-tenant association, created a new set of problems.

Another approach that also peaked in popularity in the 1960s was to place issue-centered ministries at the focal point of parish life. (This is discussed in more detail in chapter 6.)

Do You Believe in Miracles?

Finally, a word needs to be said about what clearly is one of the fastest-growing approaches to congregational life. Perhaps the simplest introduction to this concept can be seen in that line of demarcation in contemporary Christianity that has on one side those who are convinced that miracles resulting from divine intervention may have been a part of the early church, but are no longer a part of the contemporary scene.* On the other side are those who

---

*This parallels, but is not coincidental with the division between those who believe Christians may still be blessed with gifts of the Holy Spirit and those who argue that phenomenon ended with the close of the apostolic age.

believe God has retained and continues to exercise His power to cause miraculous happenings to occur in contemporary life.

Under this extremely broad umbrella one can find at least five different approaches to congregational life. Perhaps the largest, certainly the newest and one of the fastest growing is the signs-and-wonders movement. Among the most highly visible personalities in this movement are Professor C. Peter Wagner of Fuller Seminary and Pastor John Wimber of the Vineyard Christian Fellowship in Anaheim, California. This movement has grown to include approximately two hundred congregations and represents a coming together of American evangelicalism and Pentecostalism.[6]

A second expression of this approach to parish life is the increasing interest in the power of healing by prayer and the laying on of hands that can be found in thousands of congregations affiliated with one of the old-line Protestant denominations (Episcopal, Methodist, Presbyterian, and others) as well as in many of the newer charismatic and Pentecostal churches.

A third variation on this theme can be found in several theologically extremely liberal congregations that have identified themselves as healing communities. Some strongly advocate the power of intercessory prayer, but most are convinced the healing power is in that caring and loving community of people bound together by a neighbor-centered love for one another.

Typically the individuals who come are hurting, broken in spirit, depressed, display a low level of self-esteem, and a sense of hopelessness. Some have been abandoned by their spouse, others lost their feeling of control over their own life when they were fired from their job, and many feel they have been betrayed by life. A fair number are psychologically dysfunctional or have severe physical handicaps. When they are healed to the point they feel a sense of control over their own destiny, most move on to a new job and/or a new place of residence and/or a new spouse and/or a new vocation and/or a new church.

A fourth, and perhaps the largest group of churches under this umbrella are those that are a part of the contemporary charismatic renewal movement or are in the tradition of old-line Pentecostalism.

Finally, the most widely criticized of the churches that affirm miracles as a normative part of congregational life are those that promise miracles of health and wealth to those who study and obey the Holy Scriptures as Scripture is interpreted by that church. Several years ago these appeared to be concentrated in Oklahoma and Texas, but today they can be found in hundreds of communities in both the United States and Canada. Their existence also is well known to watchers of religious programming on television—and that includes millions of members of non-charismatic churches.[7]

Does It Fit?

At this point the weary reader may interrupt, "But none of these approaches to ministry fit our church. Our pastor does enjoy one-to-one relationships with people, but that is only a minor facet of our life as a congregation. Thirty years ago we had a strong network of organizations but that day is long past. Several years ago we had a minister who attempted to make this into a issue-centered church, but that ended when he left. We allocate a respectable amount of money to missions, but it wouldn't be fair to call this a mission-centered congregation. We did have a brief fling with the idea of developing a stronger emphasis on small groups, but that never got off the ground. We certainly aren't a church that promises people an endless succession of miracles! Nearly everyone today is at least a second- or third-generation resident of this country, so we're not an immigrant church. I don't think we fit neatly into any of these approaches to ministry. What do you have to say to us?"

That is a fair question and deserves an answer. One response is the classification system presented in this chapter may not fit your frame of reference. You may be able to find another system with which you feel more comfortable.[8]

Another possibility is your congregation simply is drifting from week to week and year to year without any concern about an intentionally defined role or any pressure to sharpen the sense of congregational identity. That statement applies to many congregations, especially those with an earned feeling of well-being and complacency.

A third possibility is that question is at least a part of the explanation for the decline in the worship attendance and/or in the Sunday school. The church scene in North America is far more competitive today than it was in the 1950s, especially for those long-established parishes with an aging membership. Perhaps the time has come to consider defining the role of your church in this community today more carefully and precisely and to look at the probable implications of that role. That raises the last question to be discussed in this chapter.

Why Bother?

"Everyone in our church is happy with how things are going now. Why should we bother trying to identify a distinctive approach to ministry? We have an outstanding pastor, we have ended each of the past four years with a surplus in our treasury, our Sunday school is thriving, our worship attendance is back up near the peak we hit in 1965, we've been able to attract a lot of younger new members, and we have all the volunteers we need. I believe in that old adage 'Don't fix what ain't broke!' Why bother with all this nonsense about various approaches to ministry?"

One response is that ancient admonition from Plato's *Apology*, "The unexamined life is not worth living."

A second can be found in the conclusion of Page Smith, "The man with a system, however inadequate it may ultimately turn out to be, has a vast advantage over a systemless rival, however brilliant."[9]

A third, and some will argue the critical reason to use some kind of system that classifies churches, is in ministerial placement. Historically the two most widely used systems for ministerial placement have been (a) denominational affiliation and (b) geographical location of the meeting place. At least 98 percent of all searches for a new pastor are limited to candidates affiliated with that denominational family. The big exceptions today consists of that rapidly growing number of nondenominational or independent churches and those evangelical and charismatic churches that are more interested in a good match than in credentials plus a few federated churches.

Likewise the traditional categories of "rural" or "urban" or "inner city" or "county-seat town" or "downtown" or "farming community" or "suburban" or "small town" have become too imprecise to be of much value.

More and more of the very large congregations are using size as the critical variable in classifying churches and are limiting their search, for a new senior minister and for program staff members, to persons who have had at least several years' experience in a very large church. The size of the crowd that gathers to worship God on Sunday morning is an excellent predictor of both the characteristics of that parish and of what its staff needs.[10]

The point of this is the congregation seeking a new pastor would be well advised to search for a minister who will bring the skills, experiences, and orientation appropriate for that approach to ministry. Thus the pulpit nominating committee seeking to reinforce and expand the organizational life of that parish would be well advised to seek a new pastor with the skills, experience, and interest in making that happen rather than a candidate who prefers the one-to-one relational approach or the one who is convinced the top priority should be on issue-centered ministries and social action or on nurturing small groups.

Likewise denominational officials who recommend candidates will benefit from a consistent and relevant system for identifying and affirming the differences among congregations and matching those needs with the gifts of potential candidates.

Fourth, a relevant system for classifying churches by their distinctive characteristics provides a useful frame of reference for responding to the question, Why are there two churches of the same denomination on opposite sides of the street at that intersection?

The simpler answer to that question in Lutheran, United Methodist, Presbyterian, and United Church of Christ circles often is, "That is the result of the merger. When those meetinghouses were built many years ago, those two congregations represented two different denominations."

A more meaningful answer for today's church shopper could be, "That one is really a caring fellowship built around a network of one-to-one relationships with the pastor at the center of that network while the other one is much larger and offers an extensive and varied weekday program."

A fifth value in a carefully thought-out conceptual framework for classifying churches is in new church development. Too often the number-one criterion for choosing a meeting place for a new mission is to make sure it will be several miles from the property owned by long-established congregations of that same denomination. This is based in part on the obsolete notion that people walk to church and in part on the simple political reality that most of the leaders of long-established congregations will not support the planting of new missions that they fear may be competition for future members.

This second factor is contrary to the evidence that indicates Protestant congregations are more likely to grow in numbers if they have competition from churches of their own denomination than if they represent a monopoly for their denomination in that general community. It also is contrary to the evidence that states that the success of a new mission is more dependent on an attractive, visible, and accessible location than on being located many miles from the meeting place of existing churches.

A simple example of this is that hundred-year-old congregation in what is now exurbia that is organized around one family tree or around a network of one-to-one relationships with the pastor at the hub. The denominational presence in that community can be strengthened, not fragmented, by organizing a new congregation if that new parish has been designed to produce an extensive organizational life or with a strong liturgical approach to the ministry of Word and Sacrament, even if the meeting place for that new mission is only a few hundred yards down the road.

Overlapping that is the simple, but largely ignored fact of life that the approach to ministry will be far more influential than population trends in determining whether a particular congregation will experience numerical growth. In fact, at least a half-dozen factors are more influential than population growth or decline in determining church growth.[11] High on that list is the approach to ministry.

A seventh benefit from a good classification is in diagnosing why congregations reach a certain size and then level off on a plateau. A common example is the new mission that is organized around the magnetic personality of that gregarious, personable, and extroverted mission developer who is an exceptionally productive worker. Within months after that first worship service attendance exceeds two hundred. After a few more years, when the average attendance at worship is approaching three hundred, that exhausted mission developer leaves.

In one scenario the less skilled and less productive successor perpetrates that one-to-one relational approach to ministry and the congregation plateaued with an average attendance of 125–145, a full work load for the typical pastor following that approach. In another scenario the successor is committed to replacing that one-to-one approach with a network of small groups and eventually the congregation levels off on a plateau that may be as low as 85 on the typical Sunday morning to as high as 350, depending on the competence of that successor in creating and nurturing that network of small groups and on the skills of the program staff.

By contrast, a new mission founded the same year, but following a seven-day-a-week strong program approach, may now be averaging seven hundred or more at worship with several program specialists on the staff.

While they may be of interest to fewer readers, a relevant system for the classification of churches should be used by anyone advocating the merger of congregations. Too often mergers have been attempted without regard to the differences between the congregations. The usual result is 3 + 4 = 2 or 3. A few years following the merger, the new congregation is about the same size as the larger of the two.[12]

If a small parish that is basically built around one family tree is merged with a congregation that follows the one-to-one relational approach, it may be advisable to choose a third approach as the central organizing principle for the new merged church. Obviously the merger has rendered obsolete the one-family-tree concept. The pastor may find it impossible to maintain that required larger network of one-to-one relationships. It may be wise for the new merged church to seek a new pastor who can help create a strong organizational life or who will provide the leadership for greatly expanding the program or has the skills required for the nurturing of a series of small groups. The best strategy for a congregational merger is to bring three or four small congregations together with a widely shared vision of building an extensive seven-day-a-week program as a non-geographical parish that also constructs a new building at a new site at a new location to house that varied program. Experience suggests it is extremely difficult to build the new merged church around issue-centered ministries or around a landlord role without the loss of many people.

For many parish leaders the most revealing use of a relevant classification system will be by that ad hoc study committee sometimes referred to as "The Future's Committee" or "The Long-Range Planning Committee." This conceptual framework can be valuable in (a) enabling the members of that committee to agree on a single version of contemporary reality, (b) identifying the approach to ministry the members conclude will be appropriate for this congregation five years hence, and (c) spelling out in detail the steps that will be required to change from the current approach to the recommended approach.

One example is the one-family-tree congregation in a small town that is now experiencing an influx of scores of younger families. Should we maintain the status quo and repel the newcomers? Or should we invite them, accept them, and let them determine the future role of our church? Or should we plan for and initiate a new role and invite the newcomers to help pioneer that new role?

A second example is the century-old congregation in the central city or in an older suburb that has evolved from the immigrant church of 1891 into a parish with several strong organizations and more recently has begun to shrink in numbers as the members moved away. For several years a network of one-to-one relationships with a beloved pastor was the basic approach to congregational life. This may have been followed by a landlord role in which several social welfare ministries and agencies are now housed in that aging building.

This conceptual framework may help the members of that ad hoc study committee understand the past more clearly and also identify alternative scenarios for the future. A useful beginning point may be to use a similar classification system in reviewing the history of neighboring churches. This "practice" will make it easier for these congregational leaders to analyze their own situation.

A completely different conceptual framework may be needed, however, if the goal becomes one of "strengthening the sense of community in our parish." That raises a new set of questions and calls for a new chapter.

Notes

1. Changes in that denominational context are described in A. James Reichley, *Religion in American Public Life* (Washington, D.C.: The Brookings Institution, 1985); Douglas W. Johnson and Alan K. Waltz, *Facts and Possibilities* (Nashville: Abingdon Press, 1987); Richard G. Hutcheson, Jr., *Mainline Churches and the Evangelicals* (Atlanta: John Knox Press, 1981); Jerry White, *The Church and the Parachurch* (Portland, Ore.: Multnomah Press, 1983); Wade Clark Roof and William McKinney, *America Mainline Religion: Its Changing Shape of the Religious Establishment* (New Brunswick, N.J.: Rutgers University Press, 1987); Robert L. Wilson, *Biases and Blind Spots* (Wilmore, Ky.: Bristol Books, 1988); and Lyle E. Schaller, *It' a Different World* (Nashville: Abingdon Press, 1987), pp. 50-99.

2. The popularity of the leader who is perceived as a sensitive, caring, concerned, and loving person is illustrated by the responses of public school students, grades four through twelve, when they were asked, "What do you admire most about that teacher you admire and would like to be like?" "Caring and sensitive" was identified as the most admired trait by 29 percent while only 15 percent lifted up as the most admirable trait, "teaching skills and the ability to make the class interesting" and 13 percent picked "intelligence." Louis Genevie, et al. *The Metropolitan Life Survey of the American Teacher 1988* (New York: Louis Harris & Associates, 1989).

3. For a detailed examination of the contemporary costs of pastoral leadership, see Dean Hoge, Jackson W. Carroll, and Francis K. Scheets, *Patterns of Parish Leadership: Costs and Effectiveness in Four Denominations* (Kansas City, Mo.: Sheed & Ward, 1988).

4. A historical review of twentieth-century criticisms of the Western approach to foreign missions is William R. Hutchison, *Errand to the World* (Chicago: University of Chicago Press, 1987).

5. Two useful books on the role of the adult Sunday school are Warren J. Hartman, *Five Audiences* (Nashville: Abingdon Press, 1987) and Dick Murray, *Strengthening the Adult Sunday School Class* (Nashville: Abingdon Press, 1981).

6. Among the more accessible accounts of this manifestation of contemporary Christianity are Ken Sarles, "An Appraisal of the

Signs and Wonders Movement," *Bibliotheca Sacra,* vol. 145, 55, January-March 1988, pp. 57-82; C. Peter Wagner, "The Third Wave Goes Public," *Christian Life,* January 1986, pp. 61-67; Tim Stafford, "Testing the Wine from John Wimber's Vineyard," *Christianity Today,* August 8, 1986, pp. 17-22; John Wimber and Keven Springer, *Power Evangelism* (New York: Harper & Row, 1986); "An Interview with John Wimber," *Bridge Builder,* May/June 1988, pp. 23-26.

7. D. R. McConnell, *A Different Gospel* (Peabody, Ms.: Hendrickson, 1989).

8. Four other systems for classifying churches are discussed in Lyle E. Schaller, *Looking in the Mirror* (Nashville: Abingdon Press, 1984), pp. 14-37 and 59-102.

9. Page Smith, *The Historian and History* (New York: Alfred A. Knopf, 1964), p. 112.

10. See Schaller, *Looking in the Mirror,* pp. 14-37.

11. For an elaboration of this point see Lyle E. Schaller, *Reflections of a Contrarian* (Nashville: Abingdon Press, 1989), pp. 96-108.

12. The frequent consequence of congregational mergers is discussed in more detail in Schaller, *Reflections of a Contrarian,* pp. 136-49.

CHAPTER THREE

Community or Communities?

W hen I came here nine years ago, I quickly discovered I was the pastor of three congregations," reflected the Reverend John Nelson. "One was that solid core of older members who wanted me to reinforce the status quo. Their priorities were good preaching, a pastor who loved them, and a balanced budget. The second congregation was a younger generation, largely the children of the old members, who had grown up in this church and remained in this community. They wanted a good choir, a strong Sunday school, an attractive youth program, more parking, and better facilities. The third, and the smallest of these three groups, was composed of people who had no family ties here, but who chose to live in this small-town atmosphere and commute thirty-five or forty miles to work in the city. These really were three factions with three different sets of priorities. Later on I discovered my predecessor had left because he couldn't deal with this conflict over goals and priorities."

"What's happened since you came?" inquired the visitor. "What's the picture here today?"

"There's no question in my mind but the biggest change is we've built a stronger sense of community. We've been able to meld those three factions, plus another two dozen families who've joined since I came, into one closely knit, caring community. Today we don't have any divisions over tenure or bloodlines or seniority or traditions or money. We're one big loving family. While our worship attendance has gone up, from about eight-five when I came to nearly a hundred, that's not what our people brag about. Our people love one another, they care for one another, and when someone has a problem or a crisis, everyone rallies around to be supportive. It's not been easy, and it took time, but we've been able, with God's help, to transform three quarreling factions into one big caring community. In my seventeen years in the parish ministry, this has been my number-one accomplishment."

On another day in another setting the third pastor to serve a twenty-four-year-old congregation explained, "When I came here eleven years ago, this was a classic illustration of a single cell church.[1] The mission developer, who apparently was a real evangelist and an exceptionally attractive personality, had built this up in less than three years to where they were averaging well over one hundred and fifty at worship. One night, however, he left for Oregon with a member of the choir. He left behind his wife, two children, his lover's extremely angry husband, a couple of thousand dollars in bills he owed various merchants—and a disillusioned congregation. A sixty-five-year-old intentional interim came in for eighteen months to heal the wounds, to encourage the members to forget the past, and to look forward to a new tomorrow. When he left, they averaged a little under a hundred at worship. He was followed by a warm, caring, loving, person-centered, extroverted pastor who apparently was convinced the most urgent need was to rebuild the trust level so this could become a community of caring Christians. Later on he told me that when he felt this had been accomplished, he was free to move on to a new challenge. When he left, this church clearly was a cohesive community of loving Christians that averaged about eighty-five at worship. His departure produced a lot of grief and at least a few felt they had been betrayed or deserted or abandoned. As I told you, this was the nucleus of that cell. He modeled love, compassion, and caring, and the people who stayed copied that model."

"This doesn't look like a single cell church to me," commented the visitor.

"It isn't," quickly replied the pastor. "Today this is a multi-cell church, we're now averaging nearly four hundred at worship, and I expect within three or four years we'll be over five hundred."

"How did you pull that off?" inquired the visitor.

"That's part three of my story here. The first part was to be a pastor to a bunch of hurting people, many of whom felt they had been jilted by their lover. As I told you, my predecessor knew how to turn a group of demoralized members into a loving community, but he was at the center of that loving fellowship. When he left, it was like someone had pulled the plug in a bathtub of warm water. It takes a while, but before long that tub will be empty. My first job was to put the plug back in the tub and fill it with warm water."

"How did you do that?" interrupted the visitor.

"Two things," declared the pastor. "First, I accepted the role of the loving pastor who enjoyed one-to-one relationships with every member, and I repeatedly affirmed my predecessor. In addition, I identified a half-dozen members who I thought would benefit from it, and I encouraged four of them to take the Stephens Series training.[2] When they completed that superb training experience, three of them volunteered to pick up a big chunk of that one-to-one pastoral work I had been carrying. That gave me time to begin the second phase of my long-term strategy."

"What was that?" interrupted the visitor.

"Basically it consisted of two components," replied this pastor who clearly was comfortable thinking both sequentially and in a long time frame. "First, I had to move out of that shepherding role. My three volunteer shepherds gave me the freedom to move on to the task of introducing both a new role for myself and a new agenda for the congregation. This was to expand the program and create a series of attractive entry points for future new members. The first thing I did was to expand the adult Sunday school. The second was to find a part-time minister of music to replace the choir director who had moved out of town. Our new minister of music thinks in terms of a collection of music groups rather than only of a chancel choir.[3] That enabled us to add an early service on Sunday morning that from day one has always included two different musical groups. We also always have two vocal groups and one instrumental group in the second service. We expanded the weekday program, revitalized the women's fellowship,[4] and later on we found a fifty-six-year-old grandmother with a strong background in family systems theory to create a new package of ministries with families that include teenagers."

"How long did all of this take?" asked the obviously highly impressed visitor.

"About six or seven years, but we've not through with that phase yet, and I guess we never will be," reflected the pastor. "What I really mean, I guess, is that after concentrating for about six years on my new role as pastor-program director and putting together a good program staff, I was ready to move into the third phase. Please understand, I recognize that we'll never finish this second stage of expanding the program. You have to keep at that in order to be responsive to the needs of a new generation of people, but now I can leave most of that to my staff. About a year or so ago I intentionally began to allocate more of my time to building a sense of community. A lot of people today want the intimacy, the friendliness, the spontaneity, the one-to-one relationships, the caring, and the sense of being one big family that can be the distinctive strength of the small church, but they also want the variety and quality in programming that only the big church can offer."

"That's what I hear over and over," declared the visitor. "I tell people that's a tradeoff. You can't have it both ways."

"We're trying to prove you can have it both ways," argued the pastor. "This is that third phase I mentioned earlier. We're now well down the road in the transformation of this congregation from a single cell small church into a community of communities. For example, our chancel choir includes about forty-five people who constitute a religious community. They care for one another, pray for one another, and enjoy eight or ten social get-togethers every year. Four of our adult Sunday school classes also are closely knit religious communities. Likewise at least three of the circles in the women's fellowship are truly caring communities as is our Tuesday evening Bible study group and a new group we just created for single parents."

"That's an interesting concept," commented the visitor. "How many of these communities can you build within one church? How large can you become before the sheer size of the congregation and the inevitable anonymity undercut the concept?"

"I don't know whether there's a ceiling on this or not," replied the pastor, "but the church in Minnesota that we've been using as a model averages well over two thousand at worship. We don't have enough land here to become that big, but fortunately the people who started this as a new mission twenty-four years ago had the foresight to purchase this seventeen-acre parcel. My hunch is we can grow to around fifteen hundred or so at worship. That means we're talking about perhaps seven hundred people having their primary identification with this church as a whole, largely through worship, and another thousand or so who will have their primary sense of belonging in one of these smaller communities we keep creating. A critical part of this concept is the need always to be creating new communities. Every closely knit mutual support group naturally becomes an exclusionary collection of people who find it difficult to welcome newcomers. While a few exceptions do exist, largely with the groups that have a relatively young membership or place a great value on shared tasks that require more help to complete them, this predictable tendency means we always have to be creating new communities to serve new members. One example is the group I mentioned earlier that we created for single parents."

What Is Your Preference?

The story of these two congregations illustrates two radically different approaches to the goal of building community. One is to conceptualize a worshiping congregation as a community of believers. The second is to conceptualize that church as a congregation of many smaller caring, supportive, loving, and closely knit communities.

These two approaches have much in common. Both recognize and affirm the desire of many Christians to be a responsible member of a caring community that is small enough to nurture one-to-one relationships. Both recognize that when the number of participants approaches a hundred, anonymity begins to become a serious negative factor. Both reflect the conceptual framework the pastor brings to the parish ministry. Both approaches recognize the value of frequent shared experiences in reinforcing the relational ties that are central to a sense of community. Both affirm that for many Christians "church" is more than simply being present for the corporate worship of God on Sunday morning. Both approaches encounter that inevitable fact of life that the stronger the interpersonal and/or kinship ties that undergird that sense of community, the more likely that outsider will perceive it to be an exclusionary group of people who are more concerned about themselves than with potential future members.

What is your preference? Do you prefer to see your congregation as a closely knit community with the pastor as the head shepherd (John 10:1-18)? Or do you prefer the concept of one congregation functioning as a community of communities in which many members will feel their primary loyalty is to a subgroup and a secondary loyalty is to that larger congregation? This is one of the critical choices faced by churches when the agenda calls for "building a stronger sense of community."

What Are the Differences?

From a church growth perspective the big difference is the goal of transforming a collection of individuals, warring factions, old-timers, newcomers, and different generations into a single, loving, caring, and nurturing community usually limits the size of that church. While exceptions do exist, few of these churches exceed a hundred or so at worship. The pressures of anonymity usually produce a low worship-attendance-to-membership ratio if the goal is (a) to conceptualize this as one community with the pastor at the heart of that community and/or (b) to reach an average attendance of one hundred and eighty or more at worship and/or (c) to include a diverse collection of people. The exceptions to that generalization usually fall into one of four categories: (1) the pastor has the gifts and skills required to relate very closely to several hundred people, each one of whom perceives the minister "as one of my closest personal friends," (2) an exceptionally high degree of homogeneity exists among the members (they all migrated here from the same county or place in another part of the world or all are new first-generation Christians or all share a native tongue other than English or nearly everyone is related by blood or marriage to the same family tree or they have identified a common enemy), (3) it is a nondenominational church composed almost entirely of people reared in the Roman Catholic Church, or (4) nearly everyone sees most of the other members several times a week outside of church.

By contrast, the church that has chosen to be a community of communities and has been able to implement that goal faces only a few barriers in regard to numerical growth. These usually are land, meeting space, and competent staff—and every one of those barriers can be hurdled given the desire to do so.

From a ministerial perspective the big difference is in role. The more popular choice, as described in chapter 2, is to be at the hub of that community built largely around one-to-one relationships. The most demanding and far more difficult role is for the pastor to choose to create a community of communities. Instead of doing it, the critical responsibility of the minister is to make it happen. One of the many reasons this is an extremely difficult role to delineate and fill is that the vast majority of the members want the pastor to be at the heart of that network of one-to-one relationships. A second reason is many ministers also prefer that. A third is few ministers have enjoyed the rigorous training required to build, nurture, staff, and support that concept of a congregation as a network of communities.

From a staffing perspective, the concept of building a community of communities requires about the same number of full-time paid staff per one hundred people at worship as the more common single community approach, but it does require a higher level of competence, a greater degree of intentionality in planning, more specialized program skills, and longer tenure.

From a financial perspective the goal of a community of communities is expensive. The annual giving per average attender at worship needed to finance, staff, house, and program the more complex approach usually is double, and sometimes triple, the level of giving required for the financial support of a single community.

From a programmatic perspective the choice of creating a community of communities is far more complex, expensive, and demanding. The natural homogeneity of the single community approach usually (a) requires far less emphasis on program, (b) enables most smaller churches to get by with offering people two choices, "take it or leave it," (c) demands less creativity and technical skills from paid staff in creating new programs, and (d) most important of all, does not depend heavily on program for reinforcing the allegiance of members or for attracting new members—existing friendship and kinship ties carry much of that burden.

From a sociological perspective this represents the distinction presented in the first chapter. The advocates of *Gemeinschaft* as the ideal expression of God's creation naturally think in terms of one community. Those who are comfortable with *Gesellschaft* as a description of contemporary reality will accept and affirm the need to create, nurture, and perpetuate a community of believers.

Perhaps the most subtle difference is one of scale. This can be seen in the time frame for planning, which may be three or four years in the large congregation and only a few months in the church that functions as one closely knit "big family." This difference in scale also can be seen in the program—the smaller church may have one youth group while the community of communities offers a dozen to twenty different attractive opportunities for meaningful involvement for high school age youth. This difference in scale also shows up in physical facilities, budgets, staffing, entry points for newcomers, the ministry of music, and the Sunday morning schedule.

Most interesting of all, however, is the impact of scale in shared experiences. One of the most effective means of reinforcing a sense of community is for everyone to have happy memories of the same shared experience. That is one reason marriages traditionally have called for a honeymoon to follow immediately after the wedding and the reception.

In the small church that usually means a shared experience by the same group of people in the same place at the same time. In the large community of communities these shared experiences may not occur at the same time.

"Wasn't that a tremendous sermon yesterday morning?" declares a person at work on Monday to a friend from the same church.

"It certainly was!" exclaimed the friend. "That was one of the most inspiring sermons I've ever heard. We went to the third service. When were you there?"

"Oh, we decided to go to the first service yesterday. I guess that's why we didn't see you."

A memorable shared experience, but not at the same time.

"I think the carol sing around the tables was absolutely spectacular this year, didn't you?" inquires a member of a neighbor.

"It was unbelievable! I don't see how they do it," replied the neighbor. "When did you go?"

"We went on Thursday evening; when did you go?"

"My husband was out of town during the week, so we waited until Saturday evening."

Again the same shared happy memories of a delightful experience, but not even on the same day.

The single community church benefits from the fact that shared experiences reinforce the spirit of community. The very large community of communities finds these shared experiences do reinforce the sense of community within each group within that congregation, but even more significant, these congregation-wide memorable experiences reinforce each member's ties to the larger fellowship.

From the perspective of the staff members responsible for new member enlistment the big differences are in cohesion and turnover.

The attractiveness of that powerful sense of community in the small church, often reinforced by kinship ties and closer friendships formed outside that congregation, frequently means members may move several miles away and not even contemplate transferring their membership to another church. Likewise the support of that caring community may mean most members will continue to live in the same place following retirement. A common result is the single community church may lose only 3 or 4 percent of its members annually.

By contrast, a minister on the staff of that large community of communities may brag, "We used to have to replace 15 to 20 percent of our members every year. Since we began to deliberately and systematically create these communities, we've been able to reduce our losses to about 8 to 10 percent a year. I don't think it's possible to get the turnover rate any lower than 7 or 8 percent annually."

Thus the larger the size of the congregation, the higher the turnover rate, the more important it is to maintain that steady influx of new members and the more crucial the program to enable those newcomers to gain a sense of belonging in one of those communities within the larger fellowship.

Serving Two Different Audiences

A substantial number of churchgoers want to be part of a congregation that emphasizes this sense of community. Many others do not want that or do not find it. This fact of life creates two different audiences for the churches. It also is the source of two other significant differences between these different responses to the demand for community.

The first difference is the larger the congregation, the greater the proportion of people who participate only for reasons that have nothing to do with becoming part of a mutual support group. They seek outstanding preaching or an inspiring anthem or a good Sunday school for their children or a solid content-oriented educational experience for themselves or an attractive youth program for their teenagers or a meaningful worship experience or the chance to fulfill what they understand to be their religious obligations to God or convenient off-street parking or an opportunity for their spouse to enjoy a fulfilling religious experience or a challenge to grow in the faith or a "good church" for their mother-in-law or an opportunity to share their material blessings with those in need or an excellent nursery school for their three-year-old or the chance to be involved in a non-competitive softball league or the opportunity to participate in a meaningful way as a volunteer in the church or in an in-depth study of the Holy Scriptures. They are not interested, however, in joining a caring community built around the mutual support of the participants. They express zero interest in any "groupy-group" activities and prefer to mind their own religious and personal business.

The small church built around worship, teaching, Bible study, and maintenance of the adjacent cemetery attracts and serves a fair number of these people. The small congregation organized as a loving, caring, supportive, and sustaining community tends to repel these people or to cause those who do join to feel like "outsiders" or unwanted relatives.

Few small congregations attract this slice of the adult population. By contrast, they do tend to be attracted to the high quality and extensive programming of the big church. For those large churches that seek to be a community of caring communities, this may mean 40 to 60 percent of the members do not identify with any of these smaller relational and caring groups. That is a complication rarely faced by the small church organized as "one big loving Christian family."

The second difference that is a product of these two different audiences is in staffing. Most small churches are served by one minister and no other full-time paid program staff. That means the orientation toward an emphasis on relationships or on functional programming usually reflects the personality, gifts, experience, training, and preferences of the pastor.

The very large congregation that seeks to reach and serve both audiences needs two types of staff. One is the extroverted, relational, friendly, open, forgiving, and gregarious individual who understands the value of creating these smaller mutual support or growth groups within that larger fellowship and possesses the gifts and skills required to make that happen.

The second is the staff member who is an exceptional teacher or an outstanding youth director or a highly competent musician or an inspiring preacher or a great organizer who can help create and maintain that attractive program. Frequently these people display a strong task orientation. Often they are less person-centered and less forgiving.

These also represent two different approaches to the parish ministry, two different value systems, two different sets of priorities, and two different types of gifts and skills. Thus it is not reasonable to assume these different types of staff members will be professionally compatible or find it easy to agree on priorities in the allocation of scarce resources. That is one reason senior ministers may find it a frustration-producing experience to attempt to reach and serve these two different audiences. It is easier to create and oversee a staff of homogeneous personalities.

Homogeneous or Pluralistic?

Finally, these two different approaches to responding to the growing demand that people be able to find a sense of community in church sheds some light on one of the most divisive issues of the last third of the twentieth century.

In this decade one side cites the evidence from the church growth movement that numerically growing congregations usually reflect a high degree of homogeneity among the members. "Birds of a feather flock together." Prospective new members do display a strong resemblance to the members.

The other side, which tends to be more ideological than pragmatic, promotes the dream that the membership of the ideal Christian parish represents a cross section of the population. Ideally it will include Anglos, African-

Americans, Native Americans, Hispanics, Asians, wealthy people, low income people, representatives from every living generation as well as middle-class members and also cover a wide spectrum in terms of educational attainment and vocation.[5]

This is a dream that rarely is lived out since social class continues to be one of the two great compartmentalizing forces in our society. (The second is instant gratification versus deferred gratification.)

The smaller congregation that achieves the goal of becoming a caring community that also challenges people to grow both personally and spiritually may draw from three or four generations and from different income strata, but it usually tends to act out the homogeneous unit principle in other respects.

By contrast, the parish that organizes congregational life as a collection of closely knit smaller communities attracts a substantial number of people from that second audience who are not interested in being part of a caring community. Thus the community of communities approach may enable a congregation to come much closer to meeting the challenge of becoming a highly pluralistic organization.

Those who are more comfortable with a homogeneous group of like-minded people can fulfill that goal by participating in one of the growth groups or mutual support communities. Those who seek diversity and pluralism may be able to find it in worship or by serving in the committee system or on a special task force or in one of the short-term educational experiences or in the one-day events and celebrations. Those who enjoy a "both-and" response to this issue can find homogeneity in one of the communities and experience heterogeneity in other components of parish life.

In a small but growing number of churches this desire for a "both-and" style of congregational life has produced multi-lingual parishes in which one "congregation" may worship in Spanish, a second in Korean, and a third in Portuguese, with several depending solely on English as the language for both worship and group life.

Which do you prefer? For your church to be one big loving extended Christian family? Or to evolve into a congregation of closely knit and supportive communities? Are you willing to pay the price tags attached to your preferred approach?

Notes

1. For an introduction to the concept of the single cell church see Carl Dudley, *Making the Small Church Effective* (Nashville: Abingdon Press, 1978). A comparable analogy is to a collie as described in Lyle E. Schaller, *Looking in the Mirror* (Nashville: Abingdon Press, 1984), pp. 18-23.
2. Information on the Stephen Series can be secured from Stephen Ministries, 1325 Boland, St. Louis, MO 63117.
3. See Lyle E. Schaller, "Choirs or Music Program?" *Choristers Guild Letters,* May 1984, pp. 185-87.
4. See Lyle E. Schaller, *44 Ways to Revitalize the Women's Organization* (Nashville: Abingdon Press, 1990).
5. Several of the difficulties often encountered in creating that highly pluralistic ideal congregation are described in more detail in Lyle E. Schaller, *Reflections of a Contrarian* (Nashville: Abingdon Press, 1989), pp. 13-23.

CHAPTER
FOUR

Growing Older or
Growing Younger?

During the last third of the twentieth century the median age of the members of several of the old-line Protestant denominations has climbed significantly.* By the 1980s it was becoming obvious that most of the congregations in these denominations included a disproportionately large number of people born during the first three decades of the twentieth century and comparatively few born after World War II. This discovery created a demand from congregational leaders for books, articles, workshops, and parish consultations that would help their churches reach the so-called "baby boom" generations.

It soon became apparent, however, that in many congregations—and denominations—the desire to reach and attract younger generations of churchgoers was not matched by the necessary willingness to change institutional agendas and to adopt a new set of priorities.

The easiest choice to implement, for both congregations

---

*The most notable examples of this trend among the larger denominations are the Christian Science Church, the Christian Church (Disciples of Christ), The United Methodist Church, the Presbyterian Church (U.S.A.), the Church of the Nazarene, the American Baptist Churches in the U.S.A., the United Church of Christ, the Evangelical Lutheran Church in America, the Episcopal Church, and the Church of the Brethren.

and denominations, has been to grow old together. Except for a relatively small number of churches in what have become retirement communities in Florida, Arkansas, Arizona, California, Texas, Iowa, Nebraska, Kansas, South Carolina, New Jersey, Pennsylvania, New Mexico, and North Carolina, this usually means growing older in age and smaller in numbers. This has been the course followed by the majority of congregations in at least a dozen of the larger old-line denominations.[1]

A Denominational Perspective

Two different perspectives are needed for a discussion of this choice between growing older and smaller or growing younger and larger. One is the view from denominational headquarters. The second, and the one that constitutes the heart of this discussion, is a congregational perspective.

The historical record suggests the most effective single approach by denominational leaders who seek to reach a new generation of people is to organize new congregations. During the 1880s, for example, the predecessor denominations of what today is the Presbyterian Church (U.S.A.) organized an average of approximately 200 new churches annually. That was an era when the population of the United States grew by an average of 700,000 annually. During the 1980s the population of the United States increased by an average of 2.4 million annually, and the PCUSA organized an average of fewer than sixty-five new churches annually.

During the 1880s the predecessor denominations of the Evangelical Lutheran Church in America organized an average of 170 new missions annually, the predecessor denominations of The United Methodist Church started an average of 750 new churches each year, and the Northern Baptists launched an average of 130 new congregations every year. The Disciples of Christ started an average of 115 new missions each year. The predecessors of what today is the United Church of Christ started an average of 120 new churches annually during the 1880s. The Southern Baptist Convention started an average of 335 new churches during that decade.

New congregations tend to draw most of their new members from that segment of the population under fifty years of age. This is in part a reflection of the old cliche "New organizations tend to be more effective than old organizations in reaching new people." In part it is a reflection of the simple fact that new congregations are organized to reach new people while long-established churches tend to focus most of their resources on responding to the needs of the members. In part the effectiveness of new churches in reaching a new generation of people is a result of the natural tendency of new missions to concentrate on identifying and responding to the religious needs of people. By contrast, long-established churches often allocate considerable resources to (a) the personal and social needs of the members and/or (b) the institutional demands of the congregation or denomination.

Today the second most critical component of a denominational strategy to grow younger is to encourage the emergence of a greater number of large multi-staff churches that possess the resources necessary for extensive programming. This is extremely difficult for those denominations in which the polity, or system of governance, was designed to represent institutions and the clergy rather than people. Thus if the system of representation for legislative meetings is to represent (a) congregations and (b) ministers, that naturally tends to produce a strong small church orientation. In The United Methodist Church, for example, 89 percent of the congregations include only 61 percent of those present for worship on the average Sunday.

In the Evangelical Lutheran Church in America 25 percent of the parishes account for 53 percent of all worshipers, but those parishes have fewer than one-half of the votes at syndical and denominational conventions.

Several denominations have been able to reach a growing number of younger people by (a) organizing more new churches and (b) increasing the number of large churches. Examples include the Seventh Day Adventists, the Southern Baptist Convention, the Evangelical Free Church, the United Church of Christ, and the Church of the Nazarene.

A third component of a denominational strategy is to strengthen the teaching ministry of the churches with a strong emphasis on Bible study classes for younger adults. A fourth component of a denominational effort to grow younger and larger would be to encourage 1 percent of all long-established churches every year to construct a new meeting place on a new site at a new location as part of writing a new chapter in that congregation's history. At least 15 percent of all Protestant congregations organized before 1960 display one or more of these four handicaps: (a) the location is bad and/or (b) the site is too small and/or (c) the building is obsolete and/or (d) the visibility and accessibility severely limits outreach. A new start at a new location can be an exciting means of reaching a new generation of members. (Chapter 5 discusses this option in more detail.)

The fifth component of a denominational strategy would be to repeat the 1860–1920 era and launch a large number of new congregations to reach the new immigrants to the United States.

Finally, a denominational strategy to grow younger should include resourcing congregations that are prepared to pay the price, but are unsure of how to do it—and that brings us to the second perspective.

Five Congregational Alternatives

An analysis of long-established churches that gradually were growing older and smaller and subsequently were able to reverse that pattern suggests they can be divided into five categories.

One, which was mentioned earlier, is to build a new meeting place on a new and larger site at a new and more attractive location and to launch a more extensive ministry from that new site. This alternative has been chosen by scores of independent churches and evangelical congregations. It has been less popular among congregations affiliated with the old-line denominations.

A second, and comparatively rare choice has been followed by a couple of hundred congregations. When immobilized or badly divided by the question, Should we remain here or relocate? the response has been yes. That strategy includes continuing a full-scale schedule in the old building at the old site and constructing a new meeting place at a new site. This multi-site strategy usually results in a relatively mature group of people gathering for corporate worship at the old building and a much younger crowd worshiping in the new building at the new site. Normally this is facilitated by one governing board, one set of committees, one budget, and one program staff under the umbrella of one name for that multi-site parish. Five or six or seven years later, that shrinking group at the old building may decide to come out and join the younger crowd at the new site or they may prefer to continue the multi-site format or they may decide to become two separate, self-governing, self-financing, and self-propagating congregations. Regardless of that eventual outcome, the immediate result was to reach a new generation of younger adults.

The third, and somewhat more common alternative is the one many of the laity are dreaming about and praying for—and once in a while their prayers are answered. This alternative is most clearly visible in the congregation that has been growing older and smaller for fifteen or more years. The list includes scores of churches founded in the wave of new church development that followed World War II as well as in many more churches that trace their origins back several decades or longer.

A decade after the tide began to turn, nearly every informed observer agrees the change was a happy combination of two factors. The first was the arrival of a personable pastor who was a highly productive worker and who combined creative, persuasive, and initiating leadership skills with excellence in the pulpit and the ability to conceptualize, sell, and implement a strategy of transformational or third level change. The second component was a congregational stance that was at least passively open to that new leadership and also provided at least three or four active allies from among the longtime leaders who could help legitimatize the proposed changes. In a fair number of cases this also resulted in constructing a new meeting place on a new and larger site at a new location.

Unfortunately the number of pastors who possess these skills and gifts is far smaller than the number of congregations who seek or who claim they would be receptive to that style of ministerial leadership.

A fourth, and fairly common pattern "just happened." Many examples of this can be found in the long-established churches in what once was small town or rural America. The desire to combine a city paycheck with a rural life-style brought scores of younger families into that community. Some of them joined the churches filled largely with people from their parents' generation. Before long the lifelong residents could be heard complaining, "First they came out here and took over the schools. Next they took over our local government. Now they're taking over our church—and I don't like it. Our new minister also is promoting changes we don't need and many of us don't want." Sometimes this "takeover" is followed by a decision to relocate and construct a new meeting place on a new site at a new location, but that usually is chapter two or three of that story. One price tag on this alternative may be the alienation and departure of many of the longtime members.

A Deliberate and Systematic Strategy?

A fifth alternative for those congregations that have become seriously discontented with the natural and easy path of growing older and smaller is to design a multi-faceted strategy to reach new generations and to implement that strategy. This is not easy! The price tags are numerous and some will see them as prohibitive. If that were not true, most churches would not be drifting in the direction of growing older and smaller.

At least a score of components of that strategy are easy to define. It may not be necessary to adopt every one of them, but most churches that successfully choose this alternative can properly claim they implemented at least a dozen of them.

1. The first, the one that seems self-evident, but the one that often arouses considerable controversy and dissent is to concentrate on identifying and responding to the religious *needs* of younger generations. Usually it is easy to secure approval of and support for the concept, but opposition appears when the time comes to implement that strategy. One of the background factors behind that opposition sometimes can be understood more clearly if examined within the context of *Gemeinschaft* versus *Gesellschaft* discussed in the first chapter.

A programmatic example of that potential opposition may have appeared when someone suggested organizing new adult classes in the Sunday school rather than attempting to steer newcomers into existing classes. A second may have been the proposal to schedule an additional worship experience on Sunday morning that will be different from "the regular service." A third point of opposition may have surfaced in response to the proposal to create new special interest groups or circles in the women's organization. A fourth was when the minister had to choose between preaching from the lectionary or from what was discovered earlier that month in calling on several first-time visitors. A fifth may have come when the pastor had to choose between continuing to bowl with a group of longtime members every Tuesday evening or organizing and teaching a Bible study group for potential new members who prefer Tuesday evening for their meeting time. A sixth may be the continuing battle over the curriculum to be used in Sunday school. A seventh may be in instituting higher expectations of those who will teach in the Sunday school. An eighth conflict may arise over the proposal to organize the youth fellowship around Bible study and the religious pilgrimage of the youth rather than fun, fellowship, and refreshments. A ninth divisive debate may surface when the new minister insists on canceling the summer slump. A tenth and very common roadblock is the negative reaction to adding staff to create new ministries.

In more general terms, for many congregations located on the "liberal" half of the theological spectrum, the crucial debate was over a proposal by the new minister to shift from an intellectual approach to the faith to a greater emphasis on the personal and spiritual dimensions of the individual's faith journey and on strengthening the experiential approach to the Christian faith.

For those congregations that have emphasized the first person of the Trinity, God the Creator, this often means a much greater emphasis on the second and third persons of the Trinity or on the Holy Scriptures.[2]

In simple terms, this conflict often is aroused by the fact

that the churchgoers born after 1940, and especially those born after 1955, tend to be theologically more conservative than many of the lifelong members of the old-line denominational churches or the recent graduates from some denominational seminaries.

2. The second of these price tags on growing younger traces back to the answers given by church members when asked, "When did you have your first contact here in this building with this congregation?" Members born during the first three decades of this century tend to respond, "Sunday."

Those born after World War II often identify a specific event or program that occurred during the week. Examples include that Christmas Eve service designed for families with young children, the Thursday afternoon women's Bible study group, a wedding, the weekday Early Childhood Development Center, Mother's Morning Out, a co-ed volleyball league, a series of classes on parenting skills, the men's softball team, helping in an after-school tutoring program for "latch key" children, a Tuesday evening Bible study group for couples, a Saturday evening event for the formerly married, a huge musical drama the second week in December, the funeral of a friend, a mutual support group for those involved in a painful divorce experience, a lay renewal event scheduled for three week nights, a film series on family life, a church-sponsored bicycle trip for young adults, working in a food pantry, or the invitation to help pioneer a new circle in the women's fellowship.[3]

This means a far more extensive weekday program than most congregations offered in 1953 or 1963. This also is a partial explanation of why a disproportionately large number of younger adults can be found in big churches. Few small congregations have the resources necessary for an extensive weekday program. Most meet in buildings designed for Sunday morning and Sunday evening programming.

3. Perhaps the most subtle of the price tags on the desire of a congregation to grow younger is the absence of a powerful veto group. In most long-established congregations several members of the governing board often define their primary obligation as telling other people what they cannot do. This may be a proposal for housing a new program in that building, organizing a special financial appeal to fund a public relations program or changing the schedule or replacing a part-time program staff member with a full-time person or printing two bulletins for the two different Sunday morning worship experiences or organizing two different adult vocal choirs or scheduling several services on Christmas Eve.

Ideally the response to most either-or questions will be, "Why can't we do both?" In other churches, the question may be prefaced with the words, "Unless someone strongly objects, this is what we plan to do." A third possibility is not to ask for the no votes. A fourth is, "We really cannot make an informed decision on this until we have had at least six months' experience with it." The most effective is when the leadership inspires a level of trust that overshadows those who enjoy vetoing every proposal for change.

4. For many members the most sensitive price tag on growing younger and the one the majority of congregations refuse to pay can be illustrated by three symbols: $$$.

Typically the financial cost of (a) maintaining an effective ministry with today's older members and (b) designing and implementing a program to reach, attract, and serve large numbers of potential future members from younger generations is 50 to 100 percent higher than a status quo oriented budget.

"In all the years I've been a member here, we've expected our people to carry the financial load created by their presence, why can't all of these new people you're trying to reach pay their own way like the rest of us?" grumbles a veteran on the finance committee.

At least three rational responses can be offered to that question. First, "they" are not here yet, so the current membership must finance the start-up costs. Second, the larger the number of members and the more diverse the ministry and program, the higher the per unit costs. In other words, this is not a temporary extra financial burden. It is part of a long-term process of moving to a higher per unit cost basis. The congregation averaging five hundred at worship that includes three or four generations of adults and a full-scale program normally will spend seven to twelve times as many dollars every year as the church averaging one hundred at worship with more than one-half of that hundred representing the same generation.

Third, while many exceptions exist, as a general rule new members do not reach a congregation-wide level of giving until their third year in that parish.

In other words, it costs more to grow younger and larger than to grow older and smaller. Many congregational leaders are unwilling to respond affirmatively with larger contributions to that fact of life. It also should be noted that the threefold explanation offered here is a rational response to an emotional objection—and that rarely is persuasive, except to the one who offers that rational explanation.

5. While this does not apply to every long-established congregation that has been growing older and smaller, in most cases one of the components of a strategy to grow younger means raising the level of expectations. This includes expecting regular attendance at Sunday morning worship, active participation in the group or organizational life (choir or Bible study group or adult Sunday school class or men's fellowship or women's organization), service as a volunteer (Sunday school teacher, usher, committee member) and enrollment in some form of training in churchmanship (teacher training, service as a deacon,

visitation) as well as financial support of that parish's ministry.

6. One of these expectations is for a faster pace for corporate worship. Most of the members born before 1930 were taught to expect a relatively slow pace of life as part of their experiences in school, while watching a motion picture, when attending Sunday morning worship, while playing baseball or attending the annual conference of their denomination or a political convention.

Television has trained people to expect a faster pace. This can be seen in the evening news, in the advertisements, in music videos, in the "sound bites" used in reporting on a presidential campaign, and, especially, in the best of religious programming on television.

This means the church seeking to grow younger should consider accelerating the pace of corporate worship. That generalization applies to music, preaching, announcements, public prayers, and the liturgy. The acceptable pace of 1957 is perceived as dull, slow, and boring a third of a century later.

7. The vast majority of long-established Protestant churches have a remarkably low key approach to inviting prospective future members to investigate that fellowship of Christians. Most do not have an attractive and informative sign in front of the building that can be easily read by the driver of a passing automobile. Most of these signs were designed to be read by a pedestrian, not a motorist. Few use direct mail evangelism to invite people to special events and programs.[4] Very few long-established congregations are willing to affirm the fact that spending an amount equivalent to 3 to 5 percent of the annual budget is a cost effective component of a larger strategy to reverse that drift of growing older and smaller.

The second most important part of this price tag is a willingness to spend the money on publicity. The most difficult part is the willingness, the creativity, and the commitment to design the events and experiences that will meet the religious needs of a younger generation of people. In other words, advertising is of little value without an attractive product.

8. Overlapping this last point is a willingness to conceptualize this as a non-geographical parish. Few people walk to church today. Most Protestant churchgoers do not attend the church closest to their place of residence. This is both a reason behind the need to allocate more money for advertising and a price tag on growing younger. Most, but far from all of them, come with a critical ear and eye, they were born after 1940, they are searching for high quality preaching and an excellent teaching ministry. Many are willing to travel fifteen to forty minutes to church (that journey from place of residence to place of worship tends to get longer as one moves west and southwest from New England).

9. Closely related to this last price tag is the need for acceptable, convenient, and safe off-street parking. In addition, it should be noted that three vehicles often are needed today to bring the same number of people who came in two cars in 1955. The worship experience that includes three hundred worshipers usually will require parking for at least a hundred vehicles and often more if several people are still around after attending the first service, participating in Sunday school, and visiting with one another as the second service is about to begin.

10. Why do congregations that share a pastor with one or two other churches rarely grow in numbers? One answer is that minister usually has to divide Sunday morning between two places or, sometimes, among three different congregations meeting in buildings several miles apart. That not only cuts back on the most productive time for meeting and welcoming first-time visitors but for pastoral care of the people in general. That schedule also usually means the minister cannot have an active and continuing

leadership role in the Sunday school, and this can be the critical variable in reaching a new generation of younger adults.

One of the most important components of a strategy for reaching a new generation of younger adults is for the pastor to organize and teach an adult class in the Sunday school. If the congregation has two ministers on the staff, and if both are effective teachers, both should be encouraged to teach a new adult class designed primarily for reaching tomorrow's members.[5]

Several people who have studied the churches reaching large numbers of people from those two generations born between 1942 and 1968 contend this should be ranked as one of the three or four crucial components of a strategy for growing younger.

11. Others argue that one of the most important variables is an outstanding ministry of music. This should not be seen as simply one superior chancel choir, but rather as a larger package of musical groups that may include two or three handbell choirs, two adult vocal groups, a high school youth choir, a brass ensemble, a flute choir, a liturgical dance team, several children's choirs, a two- or three-day-a-week program to introduce children to music as a channel of communication and as a vehicle for expressing their creativity, and perhaps even a church orchestra.

This should be seen as more than simply a ministry of music! A well-designed music program can offer many attractive entry points for a new generation of younger members, it can provide an enriching experience for many people in their faith journey, it can produce valuable additions to the organizational life of the church, it offers excellent opportunities to foster initiative and creativity, it can be one of the best means of responding positively to the religious diversity within that congregation, it can be one of the effective tools to facilitate the assimilation of new members, it can be a unifying force that carries the church through what otherwise might be some seriously divisive experiences, it can enrich the worship experience for everyone, and it can help people blossom as they are challenged to grow, through their volunteer work in the ministry of music.

12. Perhaps the most effective single means of increasing worship attendance is to schedule an additional Sunday morning worship experience. This should be designed so it not only offers people a choice in the hour of worship, but also offers people a choice in terms of the selection of hymns, the choir that will sing the anthem, the style or format for that worship experience, and perhaps even the length of the service. In a growing number of churches with two ministers on the staff, the range of choices is expanded by scheduling different preachers for the two services on forty to forty-five Sundays a year.

While substantial regional patterns mean many exceptions do exist, the typical pattern finds a younger crowd at the first service while longtime members are more likely to come to the later service. While the overwhelming majority of those congregations averaging fewer than eighty or eighty-five at worship (and that includes one-half of all Protestant churches in the United States and Canada) will reject this as not feasible, it continues to be (a) one of the most effective tactics in a larger strategy to grow younger and (b) a divisive issue when it is first proposed. Perhaps the most divisive single item in the proposal to add an additional worship service is the need for each service to have its own distinctive bulletin.

In those congregations where the building was designed to accommodate everyone who might come to the pastor's funeral, but on normal Sundays 40 to 70 percent of the seats are vacant, it may be necessary to reduce the seating capacity substantially before scheduling that additional worship experience on Sunday morning.

13. The vast majority of all congregations that are growing younger and larger also report that the religious diversity in the congregation is increasing. The long-established congregation that is growing older and smaller usually reports that one-half to three-fourths of all new members received come from three categories: (a) children of members who are baptized and/or confirmed here, (b) people coming via a letter or certificate of transfer from a sister church of the same denomination, and (c) people who marry a member and, as a part of that marriage treaty, unite with the spouse's church.

By contrast, the churches that are growing younger and larger usually discover that one-half to four-fifths of their new members do not fit into any of those categories. Two or three times as many come via interdenominational letters of transfer as join by an intradenominational letter of transfer. It is not uncommon for well over one-half of all new members to come in via an affirmation or reaffirmation of faith or a restoration of membership or an adult confirmation of faith or adult baptism since they either (a) had no previous active church affiliation or (b) come from a congregation that will not grant letters of transfer.

Here again regional differences produce huge variations on this theme, but typically the congregation that is growing younger and larger reports that 20 to 70 percent of all new adult members were reared in the Roman Catholic Church.

Although some church growth experts are reluctant to affirm any growth except by conversions, this writer's experiences suggest that (a) letters of transfer and (b) adult reaffirmation of faith are the two best available statistical indicators of how "church shoppers" perceive a congregation and of that congregation's ability to reach a new generation of adults born after 1940.

One of the consequences of this is the need to help new members understand and appreciate the heritage and distinctive identity of this congregation and of that denomination. This may be accomplished by giving every new member a copy of the congregation's history or an all-day bus trip to visit several ministries of that denomination in that part of the state or region or a thirty-six week orientation course for all new members or an overnight visit to the seminary from which the pastor graduated or a two-day tour of denominational headquarters or an all-day seminar on the heritage, doctrine, and polity of that congregation or a video tape that summarizes this or a ten-day trip to the Holy Land or a special long-term Sunday school class for new members or, preferably, some combination of these. This process of helping new members become acquainted with "our heritage" can be enhanced by lapel pins, a congregational symbol or logo, T-shirts, sermons, work-camp trips, sending a group to work on a mission post on another continent, festival events, annual celebrations of that congregation's anniversary, and color slides or a video tape that depict the life and ministry of this congregation during the past twelve months.

14. For many longtime members and a fair number of pastors one of the most disturbing price tags on growing younger is the reluctance of many people born after 1940 to be interested in uniting with any institution. They may attend regularly, contribute generously, respond affirmatively to requests for volunteering their time, energy, and gifts, and participate faithfully in the organizational life, but they refuse to come forward to take the vows of membership.

Some of these are the self-identified religious pilgrims who move from one church to another every few years. Others simply express zero interest in uniting with any institution or organization. At least a few want to "wait and see." They enjoy a long courtship and to some of them the process parallels the growing number of young couples who live together for a few years before deciding to marry. A growing number who were reared in the Roman Catholic Church, and who broke Mother's heart by marrying outside the church, are not about to join a Protestant church "as long as Mother is still alive."

Perhaps the people who are most comfortable with this are those pastors who rank it ninety-third on their list of the twenty most pressing worries of the year.

15. The older the members and/or the longer the tenure of today's members and/or the lower the annual rate of turnover in the membership and/or the smaller the number of members and/or the longer the congregation has been in existence and/or the slower the growth rate of the congregation and/or the smaller the budget and/or the smaller the number of residents in that community and/or the stronger the adult Sunday school and/or the stronger the sense of denominational loyalty, the more likely the sense of continuity among the members will be in kinship ties, in that meeting place, in the local traditions, in lifelong friendships, in the denominational identity, in that adult class in the Sunday school and/or in that nearby cemetery.

The younger the members and/or the larger the number of members and/or the faster the growth rate and/or the larger the size and the greater the complexity of that community and/or the faster the rate of turnover in the membership and/or the shorter the tenure of today's members and/or the more extensive the total program and/or the weaker the sense of denominational identity and/or the larger the proportion of new members who grew up in the Roman Catholic Church and/or the larger the staff and/or the larger the total annual expenditures, the more likely most of the members will feel the sense of continuity is in (a) the pastor, (b) the rest of the staff, (c) the group life or the organizational life, and (d) Sunday morning worship.

Usually this means that congregations in the process of growing younger benefit greatly from (a) an excellent match between pastor and that congregation at this point in its history, (b) creative and committed staff, (c) long tenure of staff, and (d) a meaningful Sunday morning worship experience.

16. One of the significant, but rarely mentioned differences between the stable congregation that is composed largely of long-tenured and loyal members compared to the parish that is attracting substantial numbers of newcomers is the latter has to be more sensitive to the differences among people. The former can "get by" with some marginal programs and decisions because those loyal members will accept and participate in what the more critical church shoppers may object to or even boycott.

Perhaps the most sensitive example of this is the frequent efforts to combine seventh-grade boys with twelfth-grade girls in the youth program. This can be accomplished with at least a moderate degree of success if the youth have been in this congregation since early childhood, if no more than two or three attend the same school, if kinship ties are widespread and powerful, if the leader is an attractive personality who can relate effectively to a broad age range, if all the parents project strong positive expectations about their children's participation, and if the central focus is on the faith journey of the participants. If a heavy reliance is placed on games, social skills, recreation, fellowship, and trips, the younger boys usually will have difficulty gaining a sense of belonging *or* the eleventh- and twelfth-graders will stay away.

In other words, frequently a critical part of the strategy for growing younger is to *not* combine junior high and senior high youth into one youth fellowship.

17. The older the members, the more likely they will place a high value on predictability and regularity and continuity in program planning. Examples include the Tuesday luncheon of retired men, the monthly meeting of circles or groups in the women's organization, the

traditional Christmas Eve service, which brings everyone together at the same time for the same experience, that annual church picnic held in the same park every year, and those adult classes that meet in the same room at the same hour every Sunday morning with the same teacher (and sometimes the same lesson) year after year, and the chancel choir that rehearses at the same hour thirty-five to fifty weeks a year.

One of the price tags on growing younger is to schedule a far larger number of one-day or one-evening or one-afternoon or one-week short-term events and experiences that are built around discontinuity with the past and do not require a long-term commitment from the participants. These may include hay rides, all-day seminars, overnight retreats, a visit to a theological seminary, a weekend visit to the United Nations building in New York, the Saturday father-daughter roller skating party, that ad hoc summer choir that meets for one rehearsal at ten o'clock in the morning and sings an hour later, the mission festival, three to seven different services on Christmas Eve, the sing-it-yourself *Messiah,* that mission-work camp trip, the Sunday morning "one shot" seminars during the Sunday school hour, the annual big religious drama or musical extravaganza, the twelve-day trip to the Holy Land, the weekend canoe trip or skiing expedition, the midweek revival, the softball team, that once-a-year long bicycle trip, the annual bazaar sponsored by the women's organization, or a lay-witness weekend.

Each of these events and experiences should be designed to expect and welcome strangers, to facilitate the assimilation of new members into the larger fellowship, to enhance the relationships between the staff and newcomers, to give people the opportunity for a short-term commitment to volunteer time and energy, to send participants home with positive memories of that experience, and to respond to the religious diversity within the membership.

18. One of the most divisive issues in many congregations seeking to grow younger concerns the policy on weddings for couples where neither party comes from a member family. Many pastors and lay leaders have deeply held convictions on this issue. If the objections are not overwhelming, experience suggests one of the avenues for reaching members of a younger generation, and for responding to the needs of persons married in the Roman Catholic Church and subsequently divorced, is to open this door. Those who seek an evaluation of this as a source of new members should be prepared to wait eight to ten years before demanding that evaluation and to include an evaluation of the openness of that congregation to strangers.[6]

19. Two of the more interesting trends on the ecclesiastical scene should be examined when reviewing the price tags on growing younger. The first is the very large, but diminishing number of congregations that continue to cut back on the schedule during the summer. The chancel choir is on vacation for two or three months. The Sunday school is cut back or closed down. The worship schedule is cut back to one service for the summer or (even worse) two churches cooperate. One closes in July and the other closes in August with the expectation that both congregations will worship together for two months. The pastor is gone for a month. The church office operates on a half-time schedule. The weekday programming is slashed drastically. The women's organization does not meet during July and August. The youth fellowship meets monthly rather than weekly. The Men's Fellowship meets monthly only from September through May. Literally thousands of churches have found these to be effective tactics in their unintentional strategy of growing older and smaller.

The second trend is based on the fact that two-thirds of the families (families, not one-person households) that change their place of residence during a particular year do so between mid-May and mid-September. One result is that June, July, August, and early September constitute one of the two peak times of church shoppers searching for a new church home (the other is Christmas Eve).

In other words, one of the steepest price tags on growing younger is to cancel the summer slump by running a full-scale program during the summer. A church in the "Silicon Valley" of California reports (a) August is their peak programming month of their year, (b) August is one of the two highest periods of the year for worship attendance, and (c) August is the top month of the year for that initial contact with future new members.

One of the price tags on this component of a larger strategy is felt most strongly by the pastor's family who is convinced "August should be the month we go on vacation together." That illustrates the fact that life is filled with difficult choices and many unacceptable tradeoffs.

20. "That nursery was good enough for our kids back in the 1950s when my wife and I were beginning a family; why isn't it good enough for today's?" grumbled a sixty-seven-year-old.

The answer is (a) it no longer is 1952 and (b) he and his wife are no longer the primary clientele for that nursery. A new generation of people have come on the scene who expect indoor plumbing, attractive nurseries, air-conditioning, excellent acoustics, convenient off-street parking, carpeted rooms, comfortable chairs in adult meeting rooms, attractive rest rooms, and many other amenities of life that were considered luxuries in the earlier years of the twentieth century.

One way of defining this price tag is to state that the decision to grow younger usually means more and much better quality space. Another is to suggest that instead of asking a board of trustees composed of males, all of whom have passed their sixtieth birthday, to evaluate the quality of the nursery or of the rest rooms for women, it may be wiser to appoint an ad hoc committee composed of (a) four mothers, none of whom have a child older than eighteen months, (b) two militant grandmothers, and (c) the wife of the most recalcitrant trustee. They are more likely to formulate realistic recommendations for today's world.

21. Finally, if the goal is to enable a long-established congregation, that includes many long-tenured mature members, to grow younger and larger, a high priority should be placed on providing high quality and sensitive pastoral care for all the members. This means when the seventy-one-year-old member comes home after ten days in the hospital following complicated surgery, that member receives at least two or three pastoral visits. It means when a member who rarely missed Sunday morning worship begins to be absent several Sundays every quarter, that person receives a pastoral call. It is easier to prevent alienation than to cure it. It means minimizing the number of surprises experienced by those long-time members who now are ex-leaders. Many have enjoyed the "inside" news of congregational life for years. Frequently they were aware of an impending change long before it was publicly announced. Sometimes they even initiated that change. One means of reducing potential alienation as a new generation of leaders move into positions of influence is the brief visit that includes, "Oh, by the way, this hasn't been officially decided yet, but you may be interested in knowing that next year this may happen." Avoid surprises!

Although the methods of providing continuing pastoral care of the long-tenured mature members vary tremendously from parish to parish, four generalizations are worth noting. First, only rarely is this carried out effectively by untrained lay volunteers. Second, it is far more dangerous to err on the lean side than to err on the side of excessive care. Third, mailing minutes of board and committee meetings to ex-members may help, but that is not an effective substitute. Fourth, a redundant system is better than a system that depends completely on one person or one committee.

Although this is not intended to be an exhaustive list of the price tags on the choice of growing younger, the length and content suggest it may not be easy. This list also helps explain why so many long-established congregations have drifted down the road of growing older and smaller rather than implementing the more popular choice of growing younger.

What is the choice your congregation is making? Are your people prepared to pay the price?

Notes

1. An excellent analysis of the impact of an aging membership on several of the old-line Protestant denominations can be found in Wade Clark Roof and William McKinney, *America Mainline Religion: Its Changing Shape of the Religious Establishment* (New Brunswick, N.J.: Rutgers University Press, 1987). See also Lyle E. Schaller, *It's a Different World!* (Nashville: Abingdon Press, 1987), pp. 50-99.
2. This distinction among churches is described in more detail in Lyle E. Schaller, *Looking in the Mirror* (Nashville: Abingdon Press, 1984), pp. 73-88.
3. Additional suggestions for helping the women's fellowship to reach younger generations of women can be found in Lyle E. Schaller, *44 Ways to Revitalize the Women's Organization* (Nashville: Abingdon Press, 1990).
4. Walter Mueller, *Direct Mail Ministry* (Nashville: Abingdon Press, 1989).
5. One model of the pastor's Sunday school class is described in Lyle E. Schaller, *The Senior Minister* (Nashville: Abingdon Press, 1988), pp. 146-48.
6. This policy on weddings is discussed in more detail in Lyle E. Schaller, *44 Ways to Increase Church Attendance* (Nashville: Abingdon Press, 1988), pp. 64-67.

CHAPTER
FIVE

Remain Here or Relocate?

 My father always claimed he and my mother were the first people to live here in Cedar Heights," recalled Ralph Gardiner. "They had this house built for them in 1921 and I was born in an upstairs bedroom two years later. Helen and I were married in 1946 and when Dad died in 1969, we moved back here from Lawrence to take care of my mother. She had been injured in an automobile accident a couple of years earlier and couldn't live alone. She passed away three years later, but Helen and I decided this was home, so we have continued to live here. This house really is bigger than we need, but it's good to have plenty of room when the grandchildren come to visit. When we moved back here, we joined Bethany Church, the same church where my parents had been charter members and where I had been confirmed thirty-two years earlier. Bethany was founded by a group of people from old First Church downtown who started a Sunday school out here the same year I was born. The people at first Church purchased three residential lots across the street from the site of the land reserved for an elementary school. Later on, the congregation built the church on two of the lots and a parsonage on the third one.

"According to the history that my wife helped write," continued Ralph, "the church peaked in size in the 1950s when the Sunday school attendance was close to three hundred and we had two worship services. Even then, people began to talk about a need for off-street parking. About thirty years ago the church decided to pay the minister a housing allowance so he could own his house and razed the parsonage to put in a parking lot, but that only gave us about thirty spaces. The building apparently was designed by a committee who never expected to grow old and you have to climb two flights of stairs, one outside and one inside, to get into the sanctuary. I guess they did that so the fellowship hall under the sanctuary wouldn't be too deep in the ground. The other half of the building is three stories and has offices and the Sunday school rooms plus a real nice parlor on the first floor. We're now down to about eighty-five for church on the typical Sunday and the Sunday school is about half of that. If we didn't have a pretty good endowment fund we built up over the years, thanks largely to three big bequests, we couldn't afford a full-time pastor. At least half of our members are older than I am, and most of the rest are close to my age. That elementary school across the street from the church closed about a dozen years ago and is now used as a community center, but most of the programming is for senior citizens. The last I heard, close to half of our members no longer live in Cedar Heights so about the only time we see one another is in church. The church is nine blocks north of a major street and pretty well hidden. Close to half of the houses between the church and that street either have been remodeled into two- or three-family rental units or torn down to make way for three- and four-story office buildings and apartments. Our minister told us recently that less than a third of the dwelling units in this area are owner occupied. When we moved back here in 1969, this was still almost entirely a neighborhood of owner-occupied single family homes. That shows you how fast things can change! I don't think there's much we can do about it, do you? We have to play the cards we've been dealt and that's it. To tell you the truth, I don't see much of a future for our church unless we find a dynamic young preacher who can pull in big crowds of younger families."

What should the people at Bethany Church do?

The easiest choice, thanks to that endowment fund, would be to continue to grow older together and watch attendance gradually diminish until someone turns out the lights after the last funeral. Those who favor the *Gemeinschaft* side of the debate presented in the opening chapter of this book will usually dream of and pray for some miracle that will perpetuate the status quo. Those who are reasonably comfortable with the view of human relationships summarized in the word *Gesellschaft* will have difficulty understanding what they view as a desire to recreate a world that no longer is a viable option.

The most difficult choice is to choose that *Gemeinschaft* perspective and seek to reestablish this as a walk-in residential neighborhood church. This alternative has the greatest chance of success if next year turns out to be 1922 and the use of automobiles drops back to that level of 10.7 million automobile registrations of 1922. (One reason that may not happen is that automobile registrations in the United States will total 150 million in 1992.) The combination of widespread ownership of private automobiles, the demand for choices, the transfer of the primary point of socialization from the neighborhood to the place of work, the erosion of denominational loyalties, and the greater insistence on quality have made it extremely difficult to recreate the neighborhood church of 1927.

A third alternative would be to raze what has become an obsolete building, acquire additional land, demolish the houses on those lots, and build a new meeting place with adequate off-street parking. One of the central reservations about that course of action would be the cost. A second would be finding an adequate temporary meeting place for the two years that would require. The most serious reservation would be whether this is the proper location to make that size investment in the future. Finally, it might not be possible to secure the municipal permission necessary for such a decision.

A fourth choice open to the people at Bethany Church would be to consider the possibility of relocating and constructing a new meeting place on a new and larger parcel of land at a new and more accessible location with greater visibility.

Perhaps the decisive factor in determining whether the members of Bethany Church decide to relocate or to remain in the present location will be in response to a desire to maintain a sense of continuity with the past. The older the members, the greater the desire to maintain a sense of continuity with the past. One example of that is mature adults usually place a high value on family photographs taken many years earlier while teenagers and young adults tend not to see these as treasures. If relocation is widely perceived as enhancing continuity with the past, that will be the choice of the majority. If relocation is widely perceived as tremendous discontinuity with the past, it probably will be rejected. This can be illustrated by a brief review of four decades of relocation.

From Continuity to Discontinuity

The most common argument in favor of relocation during the years immediately following World War II was to follow the members as they moved to better housing. A second, and sometimes overlapping, factor was that the new residents in that old neighborhood often represented a different slice of the population in terms of social class, race, ethnic background, or place of birth. Reinforcing arguments in support of moving to a new site and constructing a new building often included dissatisfaction with an old building that was inadequate in size, functionally obsolete, too expensive to maintain, or beyond economic renovation. For others a prime motivating factor was the change from what had once been a residential neighborhood into commercial or industrial uses. Other congregations were forced to relocate when they were displaced by an urban renewal project or a new highway.

Today the new surge of interest in relocation is motivated by a wider range of reasons, only a few of which drove that wave of relocations of the 1950s.

Today the arguments (and in most cases when a congregation votes today in favor of relocation, that decision usually is supported by several reasons) are far more varied. These may include (a) the need for more off-street parking, (b) the inadequacy of the present building in terms of space and/or the quality of the facilities, (c) the decision to greatly expand the weekday program which requires far more space, (d) the impact of a denominational merger that means two nearby congregations are now affiliated with the same denomination, (e) a fire or some other disaster that makes this a good time to consider relocation—and sometimes makes rebuilding at the old site impossible under newer and more stringent land-use regulations and, most interesting of all, (f) a decision to redefine a new role and a recognition that a new role means moving to a new site and constructing a new building.

In more general terms a common pressure behind a decision today to relocate is the need for space. In the 1950s, scores of congregations left a 5,000 to 10,000 square foot site to build a new location on a 15,000 to 20,000 square foot parcel of land. Yet location, not additional space, was the prime motivation behind many relocations in the dozen years following World War II. Today congregations are leaving one-acre or two-acre or larger sites to construct a new and larger meeting place on ten- or fifty- or seventy-acres sites. Thirty-five years ago the desire was for a better location. Today the desire for a much larger site often is the number-one reason for relocating the meeting place. A common explanation is that far more space is needed to accommodate the total program of the church today than was required for the same size congregation in 1954. Behind that explanation, however, is the fact that many churches decide to relocate today as part of a larger effort to redefine their role from that of a neighborhood congregation into a regional church. In addition, in many municipalities, the public requirements for the use of land for religious purposes means a far larger parcel is needed to house what could be accommodated on a much smaller site in 1950.

A second significant change between the relocation wave of the 1960s and many of today's decisions was mentioned earlier. This can be summarized in the word *continuity*. This may be the most important single concept to keep in mind when discussing the possibility of relocation. Most of the relocations of the 1950s were motivated largely by hopes of maintaining a high degree of continuity in the membership. As the members moved away from the vicinity of that congregation's meeting place into better housing, they found it easier to relocate the meeting place rather than to travel back to the old building. This was most clearly visible in the studies of black and Jewish congregations that relocated during the 1946–65 era, but that same emphasis on continuity also could be seen in the relocations of most Anglo congregations. In all three groups the decision often was to find or build a meeting place closer to where the members now resided. In several cases the new building closely resembled the one that had been left behind, and it was not uncommon to move chancel furniture, stained-glass windows, pictures, and other symbols that reinforced a sense of continuity. Most congregations retained the same name when they relocated. In a few cases that was confusing as when the Church Street Church moved to a different street address but kept the same name or when Euclid Avenue Christian Church moved some distance from Euclid Avenue but did not change its name.

By contrast, a substantial proportion of today's relocations are based on the assumption that tomorrow will be radically different from today, and discontinuity is widely accepted as a part of the decision to relocate. This theme of discontinuity is illustrated by the 112-year-old rural congregation that met in the same small white frame building for seventy years and is now constructing a new building on a twelve-acre site as part of its transformation into a thousand-member suburban church. It is also illustrated by the relocation of old First Church from its small downtown site to a thirty-five-acre site, as part of a larger plan to become a very large regional church with an extensive family-centered program including a weekday nursery school. It is illustrated by the aging congregation that worships in a second-floor sanctuary in a building completed in 1906, but is planning a one-story building on a seven-acre parcel of land as part of a larger strategy to become a multi-generational parish. This affirmation of discontinuity also is illustrated by the relocation of the neighborhood church founded in 1951, as it moves to a nineteen-acre site near a freeway interchange and abandons its earlier role as a neighborhood parish.

This is the question before the people at Bethany Church. Do we want to stay here and retain our role as a neighborhood church or should we relocate as part of a larger strategy of redefining our role for a new era?

This issue of continuity versus discontinuity often is the focal point of the debate over relocation.

Changing Assumptions

A third difference between the relocations of the post-World War II era and today is that most of the earlier ones were based on four assumptions that have become obsolete. One was that people chose a church on the basis of its geographical proximity, and two or three miles was seen as the radius of a congregation's service area. Today scores of congregations are relocating to a site that will enable them to serve people living within a fifteen- or twenty-mile radius. Today people are more likely to ignore geographical proximity and choose a church on the basis of the preaching, the weekday program, the children's ministries, the youth fellowship, the theological stance, or its ability to meet their religious needs, rather than for geographical convenience.

Another assumption that influenced the relocation of the 1950s was that the primary point of socialization was the neighborhood. That was where people met and made friends. The workplace has become the primary point of socialization for a growing number of Americans. Thus the ideal church site of 1955 was next to an elementary school or across the street from the high school. That placed it near the center of what was still seen as a natural neighborhood. That also was consistent with the strong child-and-youth orientation of parish programming in the 1950s.

Today the best church sites are visible and easily accessible from a major highway that takes people from home to work. When they pass that church building on the journey to work, it becomes a familiar journey to church. This also is consistent with the strong adult orientation of many of today's very large regional churches.

A third change in assumptions is the result of a combination of many factors including the erosion of denominational loyalties, the emergence of thousands of very large churches, and the new emphasis on specialized programming. In the 1950s denominational leaders were eager "to be sure we are represented in that new community by a church of our denomination." One way of accomplishing that was through organizing new neighborhood churches. Another was encouraging a long-established congregation to choose that new community as a relocation site.

The disappearance of the geographical parish and the new emphasis on pluralism combined with the power of attractive programming caused a new generation of denominational policy-makers to urge, "We need at least one large regional church that serves people from two or three counties, we need one church that is clearly at the evangelical end of the spectrum, we should plan for at least two Hispanic congregations plus one Korean church, we need at least a couple of congregations that can program to reach the baby boomers, who are now reaching their thirtieth birthday, and we need a church that can rally people in support of social justice issues." Few expect every congregation to be able to fulfill all those roles.

The fourth assumption that entered into a great many of the discussions on relocation in the 1950s was that every congregation should see itself not solely as a religious organization, but also as a significant part of a local network of community institutions. Guilt over "abandoning this community" caused hundreds of urban churches of the 1950s to reject proposals for relocation. Again this was more widespread among upper-middle and upper-class Anglo congregations (where "the white man's burden" was a more widely accepted responsibility) than among Jewish, black, immigrant, or working-class congregations.

Thirty years later it became apparent that the churches that chose not to relocate were not able to stem the tide of urban decay or to counter the impact of school busing nor to serve as anchors in the renewal of the inner city. With relatively few exceptions the churches of today tend to be far more modest about their role as influential community institutions. The erosion of the neighborhood as the primary point of socialization, and the separation of the place of residence from the place of work or the place of education or the place of recreation or the place of worship or the place of shopping, also have contributed to this more modest definition of a congregation's role as a community organization.

Changing Public Requirements

As recently as 1975 the case law in nearly every state was clear that churches could be located in any residential neighborhood. This made the decision to relocate relatively easy. In addition, the local land-use requirements for off-street parking, setbacks, landscaping, control of storm water, and building design were relatively modest. Two or three acres of land usually were deemed to be sufficient, and in the 1950s many congregations relocated to a site less than one acre in area.

Today the local land-use requirements often are far more restrictive, especially in regard to off-street parking, landscaping, traffic flow, setbacks, fenced playgrounds, the permitted uses for second- or third-floor rooms, and the disposal of storm water. In some communities every square foot of land covered by roofs or pavement must be matched with a square foot of land in a retention basin for storm water.

The net result may be that the congregation that relocated to a two-acre site in 1953 might now require four or five acres if it had waited thirty-five years to move.

The Constitutional Issue

In addition, community opposition has squelched the plans of scores of congregations to buy adjacent lots, raze the houses, and enlarge the parking lots. In other cases plans to expand the building were so bitterly opposed by neighbors that a building permit could not be secured without expensive and divisive litigation. In the face of this opposition, many congregations have concluded that relocation is a peaceful, attractive, and expeditious alternative.

The most serious aspect of this, which has become a critical issue of constitutional law, is the willingness of both municipal planning agencies and state courts to ignore a long series of opinions issued by the United States Supreme Court during the past four decades and to restrict the use of land for religious purposes in ways that do not have judicial precedent. These decisions by municipal planning agencies and state courts, and even a few federal appeals courts, appear to be inconsistent with earlier United States Supreme Court decisions interpreting both the First Amendment (the free exercise clause)[1] and the Fifth Amendment (the taking of private property for public purposes without just compensation). Perhaps the most serious dimensions of this new wave of thinking about the religious use of land are: (1) increasingly the courts are feeling free to define the nature of a congregation's religious belief system, (2) the basic assumption has shifted from accepting the location of a church as a compatible use in residential and commercial districts into making churches a special use, (3) restrictions on accessory uses, such as parking and weekday programming, have increased, and (4) the concept of "compelling governmental interest" has changed.

One result is the growing number of congregations that find stringent local land-use regulations force them to choose between (a) a reduction in programming and numerical decline or (b) relocation.

Perhaps the most surprising aspect of this increasingly serious constitutional issue is the number of religious leaders, both congregational and denominational, who appear willing to accept what often are arbitrary decisions, rather than raise the constitutional issue.

In other words, relocation is a far different and infinitely more complicated subject today than it was thirty-five or forty years ago. The old way of stating the question, Shall we follow our members or shall we stay here and maintain our Christian witness in this community? has turned out to be an exceedingly simplistic statement of an extraordinarily complex question.

Perpetuate the Old or Create the New?

Ninety years ago most Christian congregations in North America built their distinctive identity around one or more of six rallying points: (a) the nationality, language, racial, or ethnic characteristics of the members, (b) the denominational affiliation, (c) a particular creedal or theological stance, (d) the personality of the minister, (e) the social class characteristics of the members, or (f) the place of residence of the members. Frequently the first four or five—and sometimes all six—of these identifying characteristics were mutually reinforcing.

For most Anglo congregations, however, the erosion of denominational loyalties, the fact that the boats no longer are coming over from Europe, and the failure to pass institutional loyalties from one generation to the next have produced a new search for unifying principles. What is the source of congregational cohesion when nationality, denominational, and generational ties have eroded?

One response has been to drift—and to watch helplessly as the membership grows older and smaller. That is the heart of Ralph Gardiner's account of what has been happening at Bethany Church.

A second has been to build the community image around the magnetic personality of the new minister—that is what Ralph sees as the only hope for Bethany Church.

Another has been to stake out a clearly defined theological stance that sets this congregation apart from others. A fourth has been to identify and accept a distinctive role in ministry. Examples include a huge ministry with young adults or a high quality Christian day school or a strong emphasis on social justice or a big youth group or an attractive program of adult education or a ministry with families that include developmentally disabled children or making worldwide missions the top priority or becoming a racially integrated church.

It is significant that the second, third, and fourth of these alternative responses rarely rest on a geographically based definition of role. The congregations most likely to push a geographical definition of their role are the ones that are experiencing a numerical decline and passively wish people living nearby would attend.

Those congregations seeking to redefine their role often discover that visibility, accessibility, adequate off-street parking, and functional facilities are far more important than geographical proximity to tomorrow's new members. This may be the most important point to keep in mind when discussing this new wave of interest in relocation.

What Is the Best Parallel?

Perhaps the best comparison base for explaining this is to compare the characteristics of the congregation that five years ago entered into what has turned out to have been a successful relocation effort with the new congregations that were launched six to ten years ago. What do these two have in common?

The best churches from both groups usually share these twelve characteristics. They (a) are heavily goal-oriented, (b) display a strong future orientation, (c) attract a disproportionately large number of new members who do not come from that denominational heritage, (d) are experiencing significant numerical growth, (e) include among the most active and influential leaders people who want to help pioneer the new, and have few leaders who are determined to do yesterday over again, only better, (f) place a high priority on outreach and missions, (g) impress the first-time visitor with the excitement and enthusiasm in the air, (h) report a far above average level of member giving; frequently this is bolstered by the reliance on special financial appeals, (i) offer people a broad choice of opportunities for expressing their creativity, (j) find it easy to organize new groups and new classes for new people, (k) are sensitive to the religious needs of people and offer meaningful responses to those needs in both the preaching and teaching ministries as well as in the organizational and group life and in their involvement in outreach and missions, and (l) enjoy a happy and compatible match between minister and members.

In other words, from a long-term perspective the best relocation efforts produce what is essentially a fresh start in a new role in a new building at a new location with a growing proportion of new members and new leaders who are not encumbered by a desire to make tomorrow resemble yesterday. That also, of course, is a description of the best of today's new churches. Some observers would insist that one additional common characteristic should be on that list. That is the skilled, high-energy, creative, effective, and initiating leadership of a minister who knows how to help people see a vision of a new tomorrow and can inspire them to want to turn that vision into reality.

In the congregation that is relocating to launch a new era from a new building at a new site, it helps if those gifts and skills are supplemented by a far above average competence as an agent of intentional change.[2] This is far more crucial today, when relocation often is a design for discontinuity, than it was in 1955 when relocation represented a quest for continuity.

Is There a Downside?

This parallel between the rapidly growing new mission and the successful relocation effort can be carried another step. Each is susceptible to some pitfalls down the road. Among the most common are these four.

Perhaps the most immobilizing is the "post-building blues." This is the passivity or drifting that often follows soon after the completion of that last building program. This can be avoided by rallying the people around a new, specific, attainable, measurable, highly visible, and unifying set of goals. If this is not done, what once was a future-oriented congregation may begin to drift aimlessly as the members examine the future through that rearview mirror.

A second is the premature departure of the minister who served as the initiating leader. If that minister departs before new members and new leaders have been fully assimilated or before the loyalty of these new members has been transferred from the minister to the congregation, this can be a disaster.

A third common pitfall is the tendency to pay for new buildings out of the salaries not paid additional program staff who are not hired as part of an economy move. The result may be a very attractive, but empty, building. Expanding program should be concurrent with the construction of new facilities.

The fourth is the "twenty-year syndrome." Somewhere between year fifteen and year twenty-five both types of churches are vulnerable to the institutional blight that often appears when the last building has been completed; the mortgage has been reduced to the point no one worries about it; the original lay leadership has either departed or moved off to sit on the sidelines and watch; that flood of new members has eased to a trickle; the power of tradition has grown from being a helpful part of the glue that holds this passing parade together to the point that it now is a barrier to change; the enthusiastic pastor has either moved on or has grown weary; the newest new idea is now five months old and continues to be ignored; institutional worries have begun to replace missions and outreach at the top of the list of priorities; tenure replaces competence or performance as a criterion for selecting leaders; the earlier goal of organizing new groups for new people has been replaced by the effort to include new members to fill in the gaps in long-established groups, classes, and organizations; the budget committee now is more influential than the missions committee; and it is easier to hire someone to do it than to recruit volunteers.

Lest that be perceived as a discouraging forecast, it should be remembered: (a) it does not have to happen, and (b) those first fifteen or twenty years may be worth it!

The Critical Variable

Whenever the subject of relocation surfaces, it is tempting to focus the discussion on real estate, money, the guilt over "deserting" this community, the pressures for continuity versus the challenge of discontinuity and the redefinition of role, nostalgia, and the disposal of the present meeting place. This often results in the neglect of the critical variable in relocation. That neglected issue can be summarized in the word "leadership." More precisely this issue can be stated by a simple question, How are decisions made here?

This issue can be illustrated by looking again, but from a different perspective, at congregations that have relocated. One group is composed of those churches that are heavily pastor-centered. When the pastor decided the time had come to relocate, that was the decision. Everyone, or nearly everyone, naturally followed the wishes of that minister.

A second, and larger, group is composed of those congregations with a strong emphasis on congregational self-government and a tradition of heavy lay involvement in decision making. More often than not, without the official leaders being conscious of what was happening, the issue of relocation was made into a win-lose issue. When the majority carried the vote for relocation, it was assumed that all losers would affirm the concept of majority rule and silently go along with that decision. Usually some did, but many did not. It is easy to find dozens of Baptist and Christian Church (Disciples of Christ) congregations plus a few Presbyterian and Lutheran congregations that have had this experience. Typically, these were congregations with considerable diversity within the membership, a high degree of internal complexity, a history of destructive power struggles, a fairly high level of formal education among the winners, and an absence of leaders skilled in the resolution of conflict.

In a few of these congregations the losers in the vote over relocation purchased the old property from the winners. The winners used those funds to help finance a new building at a new location under the old name. The losers created a new congregation under a new name in the old building with a nucleus of longtime members. More often than not, many of the losers simply disappeared. In several cases they transferred their membership to the congregation that purchased the old building.

A third group of congregations that have relocated very successfully consists of those that displayed at least seven of the following characteristics when the decision to relocate came to a vote:

1. A high degree of homogeneity existed among the members at the time the decision was made or the congregation benefited from an exceptionally strong organizational life.

2. The average attendance at worship was under one hundred or more than five hundred.

3. On most issues the tradition was to act and decide as one great big family, not as a collection of classes, interest groups, coalitions, and subgroups or to accept the decision of the governing board.

4. The emphasis on mission and outreach greatly

outweighed the emphasis on taking good care of the members.

5. The orientation toward the future was far, far stronger than the yearning to perpetuate yesterday.

6. The regional judicatory of the denomination not only did not offer any resistance to relocation, it actively encouraged relocation.

7. The pastor not only was an active proponent of relocation but also was highly skilled in coalition building, in conflict resolution, in initiating and implementing planned change from within an organization, in active listening, in maintaining good relationships with nearly every active member, and in understanding how to function effectively as a leader in a complex organization.[3]

8. The availability of a highly attractive new site caused some members, who might otherwise have opposed the idea, to support relocation.

9. Everyone had had sufficient time to talk about the proposal when it came to a vote. The only widespread criticism of the timing was, "We took longer than necessary before we voted."

10. The pastor not only continued through the relocation and construction stage but also remained long enough to help shift the agenda back from real estate to mission and ministry and to the definition of that new role.

In other words, one of the central reasons why relocation turned out to be a happy and rewarding experience was because either (a) the congregation naturally avoided the choose-up-sides, win-lose approach to decision making or (b) the pastor did not allow that to happen.

When the postmortems are completed on a particular relocation proposal, the successful efforts usually are marked by the effective leadership of the pastor who enlisted a handful of widely respected and influential lay leaders as allies. Their vision, their skill, and their hard work are recognized as the critical factors in that success story.

When the proposed relocation program is not implemented, that failure often is blamed on the status quo orientation of the members, the opposition of two or three exceptionally influential lay leaders, and the inability of the pastor to mobilize and lead a coalition in support of that vision of launching a new era in a new building at a new location.

While it is not especially relevant to this discussion, a fourth group of good relocation experiences have been a product of a three-church merger when no one congregation represented a majority of resources. The typical pattern has been for three congregations to agree to merge to form a new congregation that will meet in a new building at a new location under a new name with a substantial proportion of new leadership coming into policy-making positions during that whole process. In some of these efforts a staff person from the regional judicatory of the denomination made a significant contribution to the process.

Two Dozen Questions

"We're not sure whether we should relocate or not; what kind of criteria should we use in deciding?" asks the member of a congregation that is trying to choose between investing money in the present site or spending even more on relocation. "Ours is not a clear-cut case, and I believe if we put it to a vote today, at least four-fifths of our members would vote to stay right here."

That is not an easy question. Some congregations would prefer to wither away at the old site rather than risk the unknown. There is no guarantee that relocation will be a success. Dozens of congregations have relocated, and because they could not attract new people, they have been burdened with large buildings that are empty most of the time. It is impossible to formulate a set of criteria that will fit every situation. It is possible, however, to raise a series of questions and issues that merit consideration.

1. Does the pastor want to relocate? If the pastor or senior minister is opposed to relocation, it may be wise to postpone the subject. Without the wholehearted and active support of the pastor, relocation may not be a feasible alternative.

2. How long can we expect our present minister to stay? The best answer is for *at least* seven to ten years after we are meeting in the new building at the new location. All too often, task-oriented pastors convince themselves that the relocation effort is over when the first unit of the first building has been completed. That is an excessively simplistic understanding of the dynamics of relocation. An argument can be made that such a decision by the minister to resign or retire at that point is acceptable if the primary motivation for relocation was to perpetuate yesterday at a new location. If, however, the primary motivation for relocation is to define a new role, then it is inappropriate for the minister to leave until that new role has become a living reality—and that rarely takes fewer than seven years following relocation of the meeting place.

3. Are there at least three active and influential lay leaders who are venturesome personalities, who enjoy taking risks, and who display a strong orientation toward the future? Are they committed to expanding the outreach of the congregation rather than concentrating exclusively on serving only the members, and do they possess the characteristics of an effective entrepreneur? These are far more critical questions than whether or not a majority of the members are open to relocation! Leaders do lead and the absence of effective leadership can be the biggest barrier to a successful relocation.

4. A strong argument can be made that the crucial question is simply what do we understand the Lord is calling this congregation to be and to be about in the years ahead? If agreement can be reached on this, it will provide the answer to other questions.

5. Another crucial question, which repeats a major

theme of this chapter, concerns the issue of continuity. Should we plan to relocate in order to perpetuate who we are and to accommodate today's members, or should we relocate in order to have the appropriate location and facilities for a new role for a new tomorrow, which we expect will be different from yesterday?

This is the basic difference between that relocation wave of the 1950s and what is happening in today's world. The answer to that question will influence the definition of an acceptable distance to relocate, the minimum size of the parcel of land to be acquired, the criteria to be used in evaluating alternative sites including costs, and the time schedule for the entire process, as well as construction plans.

6. If this is a denominationally related congregation, and especially if it is part of a connectional type of ecclesiastical governance such as Episcopal, Presbyterian, Methodist, or Lutheran, does the leadership of the regional judicatory support this proposal to relocate? Or oppose it? Or is the response so ambiguous it is confusing? This can be significant not only in resolving certain polity questions, but also in rallying broad-based congregational support.

7. For many members the most influential question is, What will it cost? Experience suggests the answer will turn out to be two or three or four times the original estimate. That should not be seen as a barrier! If the Lord is calling your congregation to a new role in a new building at a new location, you can expect the Lord to provide. Experience suggests that is what does happen.

8. For the most determined advocates of relocation, the crucial question often is, What do we do after our congregation has rejected the proposal to relocate?

The answer to that question has three parts. The first is to accept that as a natural, normal, and predictable institutional reaction to the initial proposal for radical change. The overwhelming majority of Protestant churches in North America that have relocated their meeting place since 1945 rejected that course of action at least once—and for many it was rejected several times before being implemented. A widespread expression of this syndrome was to either (a) acquire adjacent land and/or (b) remodel the building as a concrete expression of that decision not to relocate. A few years later the decision was made to relocate and was implemented.

Another facet of the answer is to ask, How long do we wait before we bring this up again and are there any changes that should be made in the way we state it? Finally, the last part of the response to that initial defeat is to ask, Who else should we enlist as part of our coalition to encourage this change, and how do we persuade them to join our cause?

9. For some the most discouraging question is, How long does this whole process take? For many congregations the answer has been fifteen to twenty-five years. That is the amount of time that elapsed between when the idea of relocation was first suggested—and rejected—and the day when the congregation has accepted that new role in that new building at that new location. If the primary motivation is to perpetuate yesterday, however, this whole process may be completed in three to five years.

10. As was suggested in a previous chapter, do the members want this congregation to grow younger, to reach new generations of churchgoers, and to grow larger? If the answer is in the negative, it may be best to forget the whole idea.

11. If the answer to that question is in the affirmative, are the members willing to pay the price of growing younger and larger? (See chapter 4.)

12. Would staying at the present site mean moving down the socioeconomic and educational scale if the congregation is to reach, attract, and assimilate nonmembers living within walking distance of the building? While a few mainline Protestant congregations have been able to move down the social scale, descent usually is accompanied by a

decrease in members. Most numerically growing Protestant congregations also are moving up that scale.

13. Is the present site readily accessible by private automobile? Does it have good visibility from major traffic arteries, and does the congregation own sufficient off-street parking to accommodate 90 percent of those who will come to weekday gatherings (such as funerals or an adult day care or a nursery school or the weekly gathering of a daytime mutual support group) and to evening programs and meetings? (Sunday morning parking usually is a less critical factor.)

14. Is the present building easily accessible and comfortable for use by persons who have some physical disability and/or who are past 70 years of age? This is an important question for the congregation planning to serve as a worshiping community in the year 2010, when the American population will include more than 40 million people age 65 or over, double the 1970 figure.

15. Does the present building include a nursery acceptable to mothers of firstborn babies? (Parents tend to be much concerned about that first baby in today's world.) Today's standards are much higher than was acceptable in 1960! This is an important question for congregations seeking to reach families with young children.

16. Does the building meet, or can it be brought up to, the standards of today's building codes? What will be the cost?

17. What is the estimated life expectancy of the present facilities before major expenditures will be necessary?

18. Is the present building air-conditioned or can it be air-conditioned at a reasonable cost? While this question is not relevant in perhaps ten or twelve states, it is important in thirty-five to forty states if the goal is to reach and serve persons born since 1950.

19. What facilities are available for weekday programming? This is an important question for congregations seeking to reach and serve more people through a weekday

preschool program, Mothers' Day Out, a comprehensive program for families with young children, an adult day care center, a ministry with families that include a developmentally disabled child, or a Christian day school. Again, off-street parking is an important facet of this subject as well as an outdoor playground for children.

20. What is the balance among space for worship, education, and fellowship? Literally thousands of congregations are meeting in buildings that can accommodate three or four times as many people for worship as can be accommodated for learning experiences and/or fellowship. If a severe imbalance exists, what will it cost to redress it?

21. Does this congregation expect to function primarily as a geographical parish in the year 2010? If so, what changes in program and/or facilities will be necessary to implement that goal? If not, is this building at this location the best place for a specialized niche as a nongeographical parish?

22. If you were organizing a new congregation this week, and if this congregation did not exit, would this location be appropriate? If it would, is this building the type and size you would want to construct? If both the location and the building are obsolete, the question in regard to relocation may be "when," not "if."

23. How much land should we purchase if we plan to relocate as part of a larger effort to redefine our role and become a regional church?

One answer is two or three times as much as your leaders suggest is necessary. A second is thirty or forty or fifty or a hundred acres. A third is two acres for every hundred people we expect will worship with us on Sunday morning. (Here again constitutional issues may surface in those municipalities in which the land-use regulations place a maximum size on church-owned land.) Thus a congregation expecting a thousand worshipers on the typical Sunday morning should purchase at least twenty acres of land.

24. Finally, what if a few of us are convinced the time has come to relocate, but the overwhelming majority of the people are scattered along a spectrum that ranges from apathetic to opposed? Is there anything we can do to move the question to the point that we can have open discussion?

One useful response can be to urge the creation of an ad hoc study committee charged with the responsibility for looking down the road a couple of decades and reporting back on what they see will be changes that will impact the life, role, and ministry of this congregation. This open-ended assignment can create a neutral setting for a discussion of a variety of possibilities including relocation. Experience suggests the second of these ad hoc study committees will be more open to the possibility of relocation than the first, but it may be necessary to survive that first committee before the second can be formed.

While these questions are not offered as an exhaustive list, they do represent the type of questions that should be raised within that special ad hoc committee that has been appointed to bring in a recommendation on the possibility of relocation.

What other questions should be added to that list if you conclude your congregation should consider relocation? Which ones will help open up the discussion?

Notes

1. A discussion of this can be found in Scott Daniel Godshall, "Land Use Regulation and the Free Exercise Clause," *Columbia Law Review,* October 1984, vol. 84, no. 6, pp. 1562-89.
2. An introduction to the role of a leader in planned change can be found in Lyle E. Schaller, *The Change Agent* (Nashville: Abingdon Press, 1972) and Lyle E. Schaller, *Getting Things Done* (Nashville: Abingdon Press, 1986), chapters 3-7.
3. An insight-filled book on this approach to leadership is John P. Kotter, *Power and Influence* (New York: Free Press, 1985).

CHAPTER SIX

Prophetic Ministry or Numerical Growth?

I just got back from a church growth workshop where we were told in no uncertain terms that in today's world a church has a choice between a strong emphasis on numerical growth and on issue-centered ministry, but you can't have it both ways," reflected a pastor at the monthly meeting of the local ministerial association. "That really upset me! I believe my call is to a prophetic witness as well as to an evangelistic ministry. The leader of this workshop claimed they are mutually incompatible."

"That's simply not true," declared Terry Griffin, the pastor of a three-hundred-member congregation on the west side of the city. "The biggest church on our side of town is Calvary Chapel. They've doubled in size in the seven years I've been here, and their minister is always talking about the issues of the day. He's forever talking about taxes, abortion, homosexuality, interracial marriages, the public school system, the city council, the peace movement, and a dozen other controversial issues. He's an issue-centered preacher if I ever heard of one, but that church is growing by leaps and bounds."

"I know who you're talking about and he sure does devote a lot of time and energy to issues," agreed Pat McGuire, the pastor of the West Side Baptist Church. "I'm on his mailing list and he is an issue-centered preacher! The difference, I think, may not be issue-centered ministry versus numerical growth. The basic point is which side of the issue are you on? My experience says you can spend a lot of time preaching on controversial issues and still have a rapidly growing church if you come out on the side of the status quo and in support of traditional values."

"But that's not what I would call a prophetic ministry," interrupted the pastor who had been to the church growth workshop. "The question is whether the prophetic preacher who is calling for change in the social structure and who is speaking on behalf of the poor, the oppressed, and the downtrodden also can have a growing church. Those fundamentalist preachers who are forever denouncing those of us who are more liberal on social, economic, and political issues may be engaged in an issue-centered ministry, but I wouldn't call that prophetic preaching! While I don't like to believe it, that guy who led this workshop may be right. A prophetic ministry and numerical growth may be incompatible. If that is a fact of life, maybe some of us should not feel guilty about the fact that our churches aren't growing. Maybe God is calling us to exercise a prophetic witness in this community and the price tag on that may be a lack of numerical growth or even numerical decline."

"I don't think that generalization reflects reality," quietly protested the forty-three-year-old Nancy Benson who was the new minister at the North Hill United Methodist Church. "I just moved here from fourteen years in Nebraska, and one of the best-known, most highly influential, and widely respected ministers in the state is a liberal United Church of Christ pastor. He is clearly a prophetic preacher, he repeatedly has championed radical changes in what is a fairly conservative state, and he has been remarkably effective as a proponent of social justice. In my mind, he stands out as one of the most prophetic preachers I've ever known."

"What's happened to his church? Has it grown?" questioned another pastor at that table.

"I'm not sure of the exact numbers," replied Nancy, "but it's at least doubled in size, maybe more, since he came."

"I would like to know how he's done it," observed another pastor. "I think he and that church are exceptions to the rule."

"Me, too," added the pastor who had introduced this subject. "At this workshop I attended, a few of us argued with the leader, and we insisted it didn't have to be this way, but no one was able to cite any examples of where a prophetic ministry that challenged the status quo was accompanied by substantial numerical growth."

"That's because most of us do our best thinking on the way home from the meeting," explained Nancy. "I'll bet several people thought of exceptions to that generalization before they got home. In just the few minutes we've been sitting here at lunch, I've thought of two more churches with prophetic ministers who are forever challenging the status quo, but also are experiencing significant growth."

"If that's so, I would like to know the secret," challenged Pat McGuire.

What Is the Secret?

The Reverend Mrs. Nancy Benson is right. Scores of churches have demonstrated that a powerful prophetic ministry and numerical growth are not incompatible. Dozens of famous preachers of the middle third of the twentieth century demonstrated it can be done. It also is happening all across the North American continent during this last third of the twentieth century. It is not automatically an either-or choice. The success stories, however, usually reflect one or more of these seven strategies or approaches to issue-centered ministries.

First, and most critical, as was pointed out in chapter 2, the emphasis on issue-centered ministries is not the central or only approach to ministry. Those churches that are experiencing a significant rate of numerical growth and also have an earned reputation for a prophetic ministry invariably implement a multi-faceted approach to ministry.

Second, as Pat McGuire pointed out in the opening paragraphs of this chapter, it is relatively easy to rally people to what is perceived as support of the status quo. The most ancient and most effective of all organizing principles for turning a collection of strangers into a closely knit, unified, and cohesive group is to identify an enemy and rally the people to hate that enemy.

Although this is a widely used tactic by scores of preachers, it must be remembered that Jesus taught us to love our enemies. Therefore, that organizing tactic is off limits to those who claim to be followers of Jesus.

Third, and from a more constructive perspective, is the most critical variable. With rare exceptions, the ministers who enjoy the greatest freedom in the exercise of a prophetic ministry first meet the religious needs of the people. That, not the prophetic ministry, is the primary reason behind that numerical growth. With some it is a steady diet of inspiring Bible preaching. In others, the prophetic ministry is supported by that extensive and carefully nurtured organizational life. In hundreds, perhaps thousands of smaller churches, a long-tenured minister has earned the right to be the local liberal voice on issues *after* providing many, many months of high quality and meaningful pastoral care to people in need. The best shepherds earn this freedom. Others earn that freedom by their simple, visible, impressive, contagious, joy-filled, and steadfast faith as Christians. Freedom of the pulpit is less likely to encounter opposition when it is earned than when it is taken as a given through a denominational edict.

To use the words of James Glasse, "They pay the rent."[1] After the minister has paid that monthly rent of fulfilling his or her preaching, teaching, administrative, and pastoral responsibilities, most congregations are willing to grant the use of some of that discretionary time for prophetic ministries.

Fourth, while exceptions do exist, most of the prophetic preachers who also are experiencing numerical growth in their congregations are warm, sincere, personable, outgoing, gregarious, psychologically well-adjusted, mature, and attractive human beings. A significant number of members may violently disagree with most of those prophetic statements uttered by that preacher, but they strongly support the privilege of a free pulpit for their good friend.

Fifth, scores of the outstanding prophetic preachers of today are readily forgiven their radical positions on controversial issues because (a) their number-one competence is in conducting funerals and/or (b) they are married to a charming spouse with an open and winsome personality who disarms all opposition and/or (c) through the exercise of their skills as transformational leaders they have led that congregation out of a serious emergency into a new era of health and vitality and/or (d) they followed a pastor who was a total disaster or an absolute mismatch to what that congregation needed at that time and the grateful people grant the highly competent successor complete freedom.

Sixth, many of the churches with an earned reputation for an outstanding prophetic ministry utilize a more sophisticated approach that is built on three critical principles. The most significant is the primary responsibility for responding to a specific social need or issue is lodged, not in the preacher or the pulpit, but in a task force or commission or committee. The pulpit reinforces the prophetic ministry of this task force.

The second component of this three-part strategy is to

avoid diversionary conflicts over priorities by asking each task force or ad hoc committee to be responsible for only one issue. Thus one task force may concentrate its efforts on alleviating world hunger, another is an advocate of fair housing ordinances and practices, a third may focus on drugs, a fourth may concentrate its resources on reform of the state legislature, a fifth on abortion, a sixth on sheltering the homeless, a seventh may work for human rights through Amnesty International, an eighth may focus on world peace, while another group battles against pornography. Those who are convinced the most pressing issue for the churches is world peace can devote their energies to that cause while those who believe the top priority should be on feeding the hungry can work on that committee or task force. This single-issue focus for each committee not only avoids battles over priorities, it also brings together people with similar values who often recruit new allies for their cause, some of whom eventually will unite with that congregation.

In at least a couple of denominational families, this part of the larger goal to encourage congregations to engage in issue-centered ministries is undermined by a polity that requires all those controversial and divisive issues be assigned to a single standing committee. This makes sense only if (a) it is true that every member of every congregation shares the same value system and will agree with all other members on every issue as well as on the priorities to be followed in tackling various issues or (b) if it can be safely assumed that every congregational committee assigned the responsibility for issue-centered ministries will adhere to and follow the denominational position on every issue or (c) the real intent of the polity is to discourage congregational involvement in issue-centered ministries.

The last of these three tactics is one that divides the clergy. Instead of the pastor being the highly visible leader for every cause addressed by that congregation, this approach is based on the assumption that the laity can provide most or all of the necessary leadership. Instead of doing it, the pastor helps make it happen. Sometimes this means staying out of the way! Those ministers who are convinced a truly prophetic ministry requires the pastor to be the initiating and controlling leader on every issue find this to be unacceptable.

Finally, several numerically growing congregations with an earned long-term reputation as active leaders in issue-centered ministries have followed the strategy of always doing this as part of an intercongregational coalition. In responding to the needs of the homeless, they participate in a coalition with three or four or five other like-minded churches. In responding to the issue of abortion, they participate in another coalition drawn together around a common stance on that issue. In responding to the call for world peace, they join another coalition. In responding to the call for racial justice, they participate in what may be a larger and geographically more diverse coalition.

In each case the legitimacy of that congregation's involvement in that issue is not solely dependent on the pastor's leadership. It is also legitimatized by the involvement of other congregations in that coalition. In addition to minimizing the possibilities that this will be a divisive or immobilizing issue in that one congregation, this approach also greatly increases the possibilities of an effective witness.

While these are not offered as a complete and exhaustive list of strategies on how a congregation can combine a prophetic voice with numerical growth, they do illustrate how it is being done. The real choice is *not* between numerical growth and a prophetic voice. The choice that has far-reaching consequences is in the choice of strategy and tactics. That choice may or may not be compatible with numerical growth. Who makes that choice in your congregation?

Note

1. James D. Glasse, *Putting It Together in the Parish* (Nashville: Abingdon Press, 1972), pp. 53-61.

CHAPTER
SEVEN

Choices for Old First Church Downtown

This has always been the flagship church for our denomination in this part of the state," explained one of the most influential and widely respected leaders at First Church. "Three out of our last five pastors have been elected to important offices in this denomination. Because we're a downtown church this congregation includes a disproportionately large number of community leaders and board members from a wide range of philanthropic and charitable organizations. My guess is our membership includes a larger number of physicians, CEOs, lawyers, accountants, and university faculty and administrators than any two other churches in this part of the state. While some of our people flinch when this is said out loud, we are the prestige church. This is where you'll find the biggest concentration of movers and shakers on the typical Sunday morning. Three months ago our senior minister, who has been with us for nearly nineteen years now, announced that next September 30 will be his last day here. He is retiring and he and his wife plan to move to Roswell, New Mexico, because of her health. I've been asked to chair a long-range planning committee that is charged with the responsibility for suggesting our next steps including the selection of a successor. What are the choices before us?"

Three preliminary comments can be offered before

looking at a range of possible choices. The first, which is contrary to the conventional wisdom of the 1960s and 1970s, is that in many cities "Old First Church Downtown" has turned out to have a bright future. Scores of these churches are larger and stronger, display a greater degree of vitality, and are more influential than ever before in their history. Examples can be found in all parts of the continent (perhaps least visible in New England) and the denominational labels include Presbyterian, Lutheran, United Church of Christ, Baptist, United Methodist, Episcopal, and many others.

Second, few will disagree the personality, competence, energy, and vision of the senior minister is the most influential single variable in determining what will happen in the years ahead.[1]

Third, nearly every student of the ecclesiastical scene will agree that Old First Church Downtown finds itself in a more competitive world for future new members than ever before.

The Choice of a Senior Minister

If the congregation is faced with finding a new senior minister, that automatically moves to the top of the agenda and is the most critical choice that will be made in shaping the future of this congregation. Among the many criteria to be used by the committee searching for the new senior minister, a half dozen deserve special attention.

For many congregations high on that list of criteria will be to decide whether the role of community leader is important. In many, *but not all,* of those downtown churches that are experiencing a new era filled with enthusiasm, vigor, a powerful community witness, numerical growth, and a strong future-orientation, several of the leaders attribute this, at least in part, to the role of the senior minister as a community leader. They point with pride to the fact that their new pastor has earned a reputation as a respected, highly visible, and influential leader in that community. They usually add that in their opinion this has been a significant reason behind that flood of new members.

A second criterion, which will be discussed in more detail later, may be to find a new senior minister who is comfortable and effective in the use of television as a channel for communicating the faith.

Dozens of pulpit search committees look back and lift up the importance of a third criterion. This was the decision to limit their search largely or entirely to ministers who had enjoyed several years of effective ministry in a larger congregation. The point was to find a new pastor who understood the dynamics of congregational life in a large church, who had enjoyed several fruitful years working in a multiple-staff situation, and who would not be intimidated or immobilized by the complexities that go with size. This criterion usually is given the greatest weight in retrospect in those downtown churches in which a large and varied program has been the central factor in reaching a new generation of members. Almost invariably that success story is a product of the efforts of a skilled, enthusiastic, creative, compatible, and highly productive program staff. Frequently that follows the arrival of a new senior minister who recognized the importance of program and was capable of building and nurturing the staff necessary for the creation of that program.

Although this may sound like age discrimination, a widely followed guidelines has been to limit the list of candidates to ministers who probably could serve for a minimum of fifteen to twenty years before retirement. This often means some highly qualified pastors in their fifties do not receive serious consideration. This has another side to it. For those downtown churches that have been in a period of numerical decline for a decade or longer, it may be wise to place competence above probable tenure on the list of criteria in that search for a new senior minister. The urgent need is to find a pastor who can reverse that numerical decline and worry later about tenure.

A poll of lay leaders from those downtown churches that are now enjoying the best era in their history almost certainly would produce a different ranking of criteria. They would place at the top of this list of criteria "leadership and vision." They are right! More often than not, that is the number-one characteristic of those pastors who are now the senior minister of rejuvenated and revitalized downtown churches.

The only significant dissent on that point will come from those who contend that at the top of the list should be "preaching." This is especially true for those candidates who display no interest in earning a role as a community leader.

What should the downtown church place at the top of that list of criteria in searching for a new senior minister? For many the answer is "vision and leadership." For at least a few it will be "preaching." For others the best answer is to go back and read chapter 2, choose the approach to ministry that is appropriate for this congregation today, and seek a new senior minister who can lead in implementing that approach.

Choices in Staffing

Next to the choice of a senior minister, the most influential decisions made at Old First Church Downtown will be in the choices reflected in building the program staff. Perhaps a more precise statement is the critical choices are in the definition of criteria to be used in selecting members of that staff. These points can be made by looking briefly at a dozen questions.[2]

1. Should the *primary* goal be taking better care of our members or in ministering to people beyond our member-

ship? Which is the higher priority? A specialist in the pastoral care of our members? Or a specialist in evangelism? Or a specialist in building a package of ministries with young adults?

2. Should the *primary* focus be on enhancing the one-to-one relationships between the staff and the members? Or in organizing and nurturing small groups? Or in strengthening the lay-led organizational life? Or in building an extensive seven-day-a-week program? (See chapter 2 for the differences among these four approaches.)

3. Will we seek experienced and skilled staff or do we see this as a training ground for recent seminary graduates and for laypersons seeking a church vocation? (Usually the best single test of the response to this question is the salary schedule.)

4. Who will select the members of the program staff? The senior minister? An ad hoc search committee that dissolves immediately following the calling of a new staff member? Or will standing committees in program select (or at least nominate) their own staff? Or the personnel committee? Or the official governing board? Or the program council?

How will that choice affect the system of accountability for staff members after they have been hired?

5. Do we want staff members in such program areas as music, ministries with youth, the women's organization, the men's fellowship, and small groups who will do it? Or are we seeking staff members who will make it happen by depending heavily on others (both volunteers and paid personnel) to make it happen?

6. Do we prefer part-time lay specialists in programming or full-time ordained generalists?

7. How much of the continuity in congregational life do we expect will be in the senior minister? In the program staff? In the program? In the organizational life? In the membership? In the attachment of people to this sacred place? In the lay leadership?

8. Who will be the chief administrative officer? The

senior minister? The executive pastor? The church business administrator? The administrative assistant to the senior minister? A committee? A lay volunteer? Does everyone agree with and accept that choice?

9. Who will oversee the total program? The senior minister? The program committee? A program council? No one, since each program committee will be responsible for its own program area? Does everyone agree with and accept that decision?

10. To whom will the various program staff members be accountable? To the senior minister? To the committee or group that hired them? To the governing board? To the personnel committee? To a pastoral relations committee? Each to his or her program committee? To God and only God? To himself or herself? To the finance committee? To a staff member other than the senior minister? Does everyone involved with the consequences agree with and accept that decision?

11. Do we expect the primary factor in determining the deference pyramid (pecking order) among the staff to be (a) tenure, (b) compensation, (c) age, (d) ordination, (e) gender, (f) race, (g) the organizational chart, (h) performance, or (i) personality? Does everyone concerned agree with that decision and accept it?

12. Who will carry the primary responsibility for what may be an unpleasant task when the time comes to terminate the employment of a staff member? Is that clearly understood by all concerned and consistent with the responses to questions 3, 4, 6, 7, 8, 9, 10, and 11? (For example, do not assign to someone lower on the deference pyramid the responsibility for terminating the employment of a staff member who perceives himself or herself to be higher on that deference pyramid.)

The Challenge of Television

If the need to find a successor for a departing senior minister or building a new staff team is not on the agenda, the next most critical choice in shaping the future of that downtown church may be the response to the opportunity offered by television.[3] One alternative is to ignore it and denounce it. A second is to produce a carefully edited twenty-eight-minute video tape of this Sunday morning's worship service that will be telecast next Sunday. A third, which places far greater stress on the minister and may be a diversion for the worshiping community, is to telecast the Sunday morning service or a twenty-eight-minute segment of it, live every week. A fourth is to recognize that television can be the most effective means of inviting people to come to your church and to produce a series of one-minute "commercials" that are designed to invite pilgrims on a faith journey to come to this church. A fifth is to recognize the many different potential advantages of television and seek to capitalize on several of them.

One of the two most common dividing lines between the curious and the persuaded on the power of television often is drawn between those who oppose and those who will support a major capital investment in this expression of ministry. The pro-television people respond affirmatively to the proposal to raise a few hundred thousand dollars for the installation of a fully equipped studio plus both remote controlled and operator-controlled cameras plus a substantial item in the annual operating budget for a visual-media staff specialist and operating expenses.

Those opposed to that investment usually favor a more traditional approach to ministry and some will contend that a more economical substitute is radio. Radio is not a substitute for television! It is a completely different medium designed to reach a different audience at a different time through a radically different approach to programming. A parallel to the proposal to rely on radio rather than meet the costs of television is similar to the question, Should we lease an automobile or an airplane for our pastor's use? Both are means of transportation, each requires a unique set of skills to operate it, each has advantages and limitations, one costs more than the other, and they serve substantially different purposes.

The second, and perhaps the more common dividing line that can be seen in the choosing up of sides over television, is really a philosophical debate over values, priorities, world views, the response to a changing society, and technological innovation. It reflects the *Gemeinschaft* versus *Gesellschaft* world view described in the opening chapter.

Another context for looking at the debate over television will be familiar ground to those who have enjoyed reading congregational histories. They can point to the parallels in earlier debates on whether a telephone should be installed in the church building (a common answer was in the parsonage or manse, but not in the church building) or whether a pastor should own an automobile (yes, as long as he refrained from driving it on Sunday), radio (it was acceptable for Christians to own a radio as long as no one listened to it on the Sabbath) and motion pictures (still photography probably did not violate the Second Commandment, but pictures that moved did, thus returning missionaries could show color slides of their work, but motion pictures could not be used as an instructional tool in the Sunday school).

Opponents of television often contend it cheapens the biblical story and it is not a useful channel for challenging people to think. (This overlooks the impact of television as an ally in the civil rights movement of the 1960s or in the coverage of the Vietnam War or in the debate over whether fires in the national parks should be allowed to burn themselves out naturally.) These opponents of television often point to the scandals associated with the televangelists of the late 1980s and argue that television tends to glamorize the personalities rather than communicate the essentials of the Christian faith. They have a case. Television is vulnerable to abuse, just as a few radio preachers of the 1930s abused that channel of communication and several of the great revivalists of the nineteenth century used meeting halls and tents to manipulate the emotions of their listeners. The doctrine of original sin is a fact of human existence that cannot be ignored.

The other side of this philosophical argument is that television has replaced the itinerant public speaker, the newspaper, and the radio as the most influential channel of communication today. One way of stating the question is, Should we use it or not? Another is, Do we feel we are likely to abuse that channel of communication and therefore we should leave it to be used by others who are more likely to be faithful and responsible users of that magic medium than we might be? Television is and will continue to be used to communicate the gospel of Jesus Christ. That is a fact of life today. Whether the people at Old First Church Downtown believe they can be faithful and responsible users of that medium is a question only they can answer.

Those who are convinced they can trust themselves and their pastor can find television to be a useful tool of ministry. Those who want this to be an "influential pulpit in this community" will find that television can be a means to an end. Those who wish, "We have a wonderful preacher who brings us superb sermons week after week, I wish more people could hear them," will find television can help fulfill that wish. Those who regret, "My grandparents couldn't be here for the baptism of their great grandchild," can still take advantage of the fact that one of the unique characteristics of television (and video tape) is that one can be there without actually being present. Those who silently yearn, "I wish there was some way our minister could sit in the pew and watch himself in the pulpit. If he could, I'm sure he would break himself of some of his disturbing habits and gestures," can turn to video tapes to have their wish granted. Those who demand, "Our pastor should ban all those people who get in the way when they video tape weddings," can have that demand met, and still produce a better quality video tape for that newly married couple with the aid of those remote-control cameras and that console in the studio upstairs or in the basement. Those who are concerned that "My mother, who is in a nursing home, misses being able to be a part of our fellowship here," can have that price tag of absence partially offset by video tapes of worship, weddings, funerals, anniversary celebrations, visiting speakers, and special meetings of the women's organizations.

The only decisive argument against the use of television by Old First Church Downtown is, "Our minister is a dull, long-winded and boring preacher." That is a severe handicap for most congregations. (Perhaps the one exception is the church organized around that network of one-to-one relationships described in chapter 2 with a loving, caring, person-centered pastor at the hub of that network.) Television does require a far above average level of competence in communication skills. It does not tolerate incompetence or dullness. (It also should be noted that the visual dimension of television creates a strong bias against healthy individuals and in favor of severely malnourished people. As long as television is a factor in presidential elections, it will be difficult for anyone resembling William Howard Taft to win the nomination.)

Three other factors in the debate over the use of television also merit consideration. First, the "flagship role for a church of our denomination" usually goes with the decision on television. If the people at Old First Church Downtown conclude they cannot be entrusted with the risks that go with television and that responsibility should be given to some other congregation, that probably also will mean surrendering that "flagship" role. Second, unlike the pastor of the small church who often can claim, "I know my people better than they know me," the senior minister of Old First Church Downtown usually has to live with the fact, "My people know me better than I know them." Television enhances this anonymity of the congregation.

Many people, some of whom attend irregularly and some who never attend, come to regard the television preacher as an "old friend." One result is a warm greeting from the cashier in the supermarket or a stranger in the library. The minister may return that friendly greeting while silently convinced, "I've never seen you before in my life." Another facet of this anonymity of the television audience often is represented by the requests for the senior minister, or some other staff member, to officiate at the funeral service or wedding of people from that living-room congregation watching television.

A third variable reflects substantially the interests, personality, skills, and preferences of that senior minister. Television does open the door for the pastor to become one of the most influential voices in the life and value system of that community system. This often is resented by elected officials, and many ministers also are reluctant to accept that role. On the other hand those who believe the Christian Church should offer a more powerful witness to the faith can find television to be a powerful tool for accomplishing that goal. Again, many members of the clergy, including a surprisingly large number of denominational officials, apparently believe no one in their denominational family can be trusted with that responsibility and prefer that role be filled by the pastor of a church from another denomination or from a nondenominational church or by a national televangelist.

The choice on the use of cable versus through-the-air television signals is beyond this discussion and must be made in the context of that particular situation in terms of cost, audience, and geography.

Should We Advertise?

If the selection of a senior minister, the building of a program staff, and a response to the opportunities offered by television rank at the top of the list of choices before the leaders at Old First Church Downtown, what is next on the list?

For many the next issue should be discussed in the context of the *Gemeinschaft und Gesellschaft* conceptual framework presented in the first chapter. Those who are convinced that Old First Church Downtown functions in a small, uncomplicated, and intimate community can offer persuasive arguments that advertising is unnecessary, inappropriate, inefficient, and a waste of money. Those who concede that the term *Gesellschaft* represents a more realistic statement of the contemporary context for ministry will support that expenditure.

"Well, all I can say is, don't ask me for the money to pay the bills," declared one of the losers when the church council at First Church voted by a 9 to 6 margin in favor of an extensive publicity program. "I not only think it's a waste of money, I also am convinced it is beneath the dignity of this congregation. We're not a discount store or an automobile dealer or a circus. We're a community of believers gathered around a common belief that Jesus Christ is Lord and Savior and that we are called to proclaim His rule, to worship Him, and to sing the praise of our Lord. We're not a group of hucksters selling used cars or aluminum storm doors. Some things simply are inconsistent with who we claim to be as Christians, and I believe advertising is on that list."

This statement represents a widely shared point of view that should be respected, but not necessarily adopted. One means of accomplishing that is to fund that public relations effort from designated second-mile contributions. This has several advantages. It avoids offending those who object to their contributions being used for something they disapprove. It eliminates at least one potential veto point (the finance committee) in the whole process and minimizes the chance that implementation will be postponed because "we have a very tight budget for the coming year and we had to cut all but the absolute essentials." Dependence on designated second-mile contributions for advertising usually will produce a larger sum of money than will the inclusion of it in the basic annual budget.

Most important of all, in the vast majority of congregations the budgeting process is tied to a twelve-month time frame. This means an annual review of each new program. (At this point the budget officer's cliche becomes relevant. "It is extremely difficult to get anything new into the budget. It is even more difficult to get anything out of the budget that has been in it for years.")

The items most vulnerable to disapproval in that annual review are those that were new last year or the year before last. Premature evaluation can kill a promising public relations program. Many churches report that the impact of a new advertising program did not begin to produce highly visible results until after eighteen to twenty-four months. Keeping it out of the budget is one way of avoiding premature evaluation. For some downtown churches the Yellow Pages will be the most productive advertising vehicle. From a cost-benefit perspective direct mail may be the most efficient. Television may be the most expensive as well as the most powerful. Radio can be useful. The priorities usually depend on local circumstances.[4]

Should We Become a Regional Church?

The responses to the choices on staffing, television, and advertising should be internally consistent with a fourth choice. Should we define our role as a downtown church or a regional church? The response to that question also will give direction to the remaining choices raised later in this chapter. Once again this is at least in part a *Gemeinschaft* or *Gesellschaft* view of the world issue. Is the number-one client the community that can be summarized in the word "downtown"? Or is the number-one client that metropolitan region? The answer to that choice will influence decisions on staffing, television, and advertising as well as on role, schedules, and facilities.

One of the factors that should be considered in this debate goes back to that role as "the flagship church." Once upon a time that role naturally was granted to Old First Church Downtown. Today it usually has to be earned by performance. The self-identified regional church that accepts the obligations of that role, regardless of the location of the meeting place, is the one most likely to be recognized by others as "our flagship church."

Weekday or Sunday?

Another extremely influential choice facing the leaders at Old First Church Downtown may be the choice between concentrating as much program as possible into Sunday or deciding to function as a seven-day-a-week church with extensive weekday programming.

One variable in this decision will be the priorities of the senior minister. A second will be the competition—what are other churches doing? A third, and for many the determinative variable, will be the facilities, including location, accessibility to the lunch-hour population and off-street parking.

A fourth variable will be the self-identified role. The congregation that sees itself as a regional parish often will have as many or more people coming to that meeting place during the week as appear on Sunday morning.

By contrast, many self-identified downtown churches concentrate most of the member-oriented programming into (a) Sunday morning and (b) Sunday or Wednesday evening. The evening schedule often begins with choir practice for three or four choirs followed by the gathering of the junior high youth group or the confirmation class, a meal for all ages, Bible study and/or worship for all ages, various committee meetings, the senior high youth fellowship, the weekly rehearsal of the chancel choir, an orientation class for new members, and perhaps even one or two recreational activities if the facilities include a gymnasium and occasionally the memorial service for a deceased member.

One explanation of this concentration of events in one evening is to simplify life for families who live many miles away. Another is to "bring our church family together every week." A third is that some individuals may be reluctant to venture forth alone downtown after dark. A fourth is the shortage of off-street parking for weekday activities. A fifth is an effort to improve the assimilation of new members. A sixth may be for the convenience of the paid staff and/or volunteer lay leadership.

The limitations faced by some downtown churches in their desire to build a strong weekday program has forced them to examine what for many is the most difficult and potentially divisive choice described in this chapter.

Remodel or Relocate?

Does a downtown church have to meet in a building located in the central business district? By definition the answer is yes. Does the regional parish or the flagship church of that denomination have to be housed in a downtown building? The answer is clearly no. Dozens of Old First Church Downtown congregations have redefined their role as regional churches and, as a part of the fulfillment of that new role, moved to a new meeting place on a larger parcel of land at an easily accessible and highly visible site. This is more common west of the Mississippi River than east of it and in the Southeast, partly because of a more competitive ecclesiastical scene in the West (and also in the Southeast).

Frequently the option of relocation was not even considered in the process of planning for a new era, but was placed on the agenda following a careful study of the costs of remodeling the existing facilities. A not uncommon sequence followed this pattern. The initial motivation to appoint a special study committee to examine the future was the decline in worship attendance. This generated the need to look at a revision of the total program. Out of this came the recognition of a need to improve the quality of the physical facilities to house that new program. Sometimes the cost of remodeling placed relocation on the agenda as an attractive option. More often the initial remodeling program was completed and discontent with the results stimulated the desire to look at relocation. That decision also has been facilitated for many churches by creative uses of television.

For many people the persuasive argument is, "We want this to be the most influential pulpit in this region, and that is possible only if we remain downtown." That not only was a persuasive argument in 1953, it also reflected contemporary reality. That world no longer exists. Today the potential influence of any one preacher is not determined by the location of the pulpit, but by the names and numbers of people who hear what is spoken from that pulpit. The combination of the suburbanization of the place of residence of many influential community leaders, both black and white, plus the power of television mean a downtown location no longer is crucial for the role of being an "influential pulpit."

Today one of the critical questions to be raised at Old First Church Downtown when the issue of relocation arises is, Do we want to accept a role as a regional church, and if we do, can we fulfill that role from this location?

Whether the decision is to remain downtown and remodel what may have become obsolete facilities or to relocate and construct the meeting place necessary for a regional church, that decision almost certainly means affirming a role as a non-geographical church. That also may be a change from a *Gemeinschaft* self-image to affirming a *Gesellschaft* role. The combination of a preference for the status quo plus a reluctance to accept the more complex role of a regional church has defeated many relocation proposals. (For a more extended discussion of relocation see chapter 5.)

Choirs or Music Program?

One of the two or three biggest points of discontinuity with the past for many of today's strongest downtown churches is in music. For decades the basic conceptual framework was to examine the quality and count the number of choirs. Today a better frame of reference is to think in terms of an extensive and varied music program that may include two or three adult choirs (one for each worship experience on Sunday morning), a high school youth choir, a liturgical dance group, a flute choir, a weekday music encounter program for young children using Orph instruments, an adult choir that is primarily a closely knit religious community and secondarily a vocal group, an all-church orchestra, an extravagant Advent program that is open to the general public and may attract several thousand people to three to seven December performances (Round the Table Carol Sing or the Living Christmas Tree are examples), three or four handbell choirs, a weekday program that utilizes the power of music to help women progress on their faith journey, a brass ensemble, a junior high girls' chorus that includes many nonmembers, one big trip annually for each of two or three choirs, a drama group that offers three or four performances of a play once or twice a year, voice lessons, three or four children's vocal choirs, and a touring choir of mature adults who, on twenty Sundays a year, provide the choir anthem for various small congregations without their own chancel choir.

Three reasonable goals are: (a) the number of people who are actively involved in that extensive ministry of music will be equal to 15 to 30 percent of the total membership, (b) the music program will be one of the two or three biggest and most attractive entry points for newcomers into that congregation, and (c) the ministry of music will be a powerful force in the assimilation of new members.[5]

Should We Be a Teaching Church?

Historically many downtown churches have seen themselves as "ports of entry" for newcomers to that urban community who were welcomed into that congregation. Subsequently many of these newcomers moved to another parish in an outlying residential community. Whether that self-image reflects 1923 or 1953 more accurately than 1993 is not a point of complete agreement. It is true, however, that most of the large and rapidly growing downtown churches do attract a significant number of new members who subsequently depart for a new church home. One result is some of the leaders of downtown churches identify one of their responsibilities as training people for ministry in other churches.

In recent years a new concept has emerged. Instead of "exporting" skilled lay volunteers, another possibility is to export skills, learning, ideas, creativity, and dreams. Paralleling this has been a growing recognition that excessive expectations have been placed on theological seminaries in preparing students for the pastoral ministry and a sharp rise in the number of lay volunteers attending continuing education events designed for congregational leaders.

One result is a rapidly growing number of self-identified

"teaching churches" that offer two- to five-day training events for both paid staff members and volunteer leaders. The need still exceeds the available resources. Therefore one of the choices open to the downtown church (or to the regional church) is to accept a role as a teaching church.

The themes for these events vary tremendously! Examples include reversing the numerical decline in the downtown church, ministries with that new generation of teenagers born after 1968, ministries with the formerly married, weekday programming in Christian education, community outreach, music, sheltering the homeless, weekday early childhood development programs, ministry in retirement communities, church finances, prayer, the Christian day school, revitalizing the women's fellowship, expanding the adult Sunday school, reaching and serving the tourists in a resort community, ministries with single parent families, organizing a mission-work camp trip, spiritual growth, preaching, church administration, and clown ministries.[6]

An acceptance of this role as a teaching church can: (1) benefit and enrich the churches from which the participants come, (2) challenge and inspire the creative gifts of those who attend, (3) transmit experience-based skills, (4) force the leaders in the teaching church to reflect on their experiences and enhance their intentionality in ministry, (5) create new networks of like-minded Christians, (6) bring constructive questions to the leaders in the teaching church, and (7) serve as a stimulating and unifying experience for those who come together and carry out a constructive postmortem on their experience on the way back home.

Who will lift up these choices in your church? Who will choose from among the alternatives offered by these choices?

Notes

1. A detailed examination of the role of the senior minister and of factors to be considered in staffing the large church can be found in

Lyle E. Schaller, *The Senior Minister* (Nashville: Abingdon Press, 1988) and in Lyle E. Schaller, *The Multiple Staff and the Larger Church* (Nashville: Abingdon Press, 1980).

2. A more extensive discussion of staffing the multiple-staff congregation can be found in Schaller, *The Senior Minister,* pp. 42-99.

3. A provocative introduction to the politics of the churches' use of television and to the difficulties inherent in evaluating it can be found in a series of articles in *Review of Religious Research,* December, 1987, vol. 29, 2. This issue also contains extensive bibliographic references. Perhaps the best general book on the impact of television is Joshua Meyrowitz, *No Sense of Place: The Impact of the Electronic Media on Social Behavior* (New York: Oxford University Press, 1985). An excellent analysis of the religious use of television is Steward M. Hoover, *Mass Media Religion: The Social Sources of the Electronic Church* (Newbury Park, Ca.: Sage Publications, 1988).

4. Walter Mueller, *Direct Mail Ministry* (Nashville: Abingdon Press, 1989).

5. A more extensive discussion of this distinction can be found in Lyle E. Schaller, "Music in the Large Church," *Choristers Guild Letters,* March 1980, pp. 123-25; "Choirs or Music Program," *Choristers Guild Letters,* May 1984, pp. 185-87; "How Large Is Your Choir?" *Choristers Guild Letters,* January 1985, pp. 83-85; "The Ministry of Music and Church Growth," *Choristers Guild Letters,* October 1985, pp. 25-26; and "The Ministry of Music and the Assimilation of New Members," *Choristers Guild Letters,* November 1988, pp. 93-95.

6. An excellent book on clown ministries is Dick Hardel, *Welcome to the Sawdust Circle.* It includes an exhaustive bibliography. For details write Dick Hardel, 1600 S. Orlando Ave., Winter Park, FL 32789.

CHAPTER EIGHT

The Rural Church and the Sixty-Mile City

I guess I can understand why they do it," reflected the seventy-one-year-old Walter Gray, who really did not understand. "Their kids want to be part of a big youth program, and our little church can't possibly provide that, but we sure miss them! They grew up in that little church and I guess we all assumed when they stayed here in the community, they would stay in our church. Our oldest boy is a long-distance truck driver, and he lives just down the street a couple of blocks. He married a girl he met while he was going to what at the time was the new consolidated high school and she was active in the church there, so I guess it's only natural he goes to her church, but it is a twelve-mile trip each way. Our second son decided he wanted to be a cabinetmaker and he has his shop in the barn on a five-acre parcel of land just outside of town. The neighboring farmer bought the rest of the land and our son purchased the house, barn, and five acres that includes a small orchard. He's fixed the barn up into a real nice shop and he now has six men working for him. His wife, Anne, keeps the books for him and they're doing real well. Even though we have a church of our denomination right here in town, almost within walking distance of their house, they also drive into the city to go to Trinity Church where our oldest boy and his family are members. My wife and I, of course, still drive six miles out into the country a couple of times a week to go to church. That's the church we grew up in, that's where we were married, and that's where all four of our children were baptized and our daughter also was married there. She and her husband live in California. Our other son is a lawyer in Maryland."

Walter Gray was describing what has become an increasingly common pattern of churchgoing in nonmetropolitan America. Walter and Sarah, his wife of nearly fifty years, retired from farming several years earlier and sold their farm to a neighbor who needed the additional land. The Grays moved into town to live out their retirement years. That community of nearly seven-hundred residents is served by four churches, one of which is a member of the same denomination the Grays have belonged to all their lives. They do not go to that church, however. About twice a week Walter and Sarah drive out to worship with a couple dozen of their lifelong friends, former neighbors, and relatives. If the weather is bad, Sarah and Walter often ride out with Ed and Lucy Nelson, another retired farm couple who also moved to town when they sold their farm, but continue their lifelong membership in that same congregation that meets in that white frame building next to a cemetery on a rural road. Both the Grays and Nelsons expect that eventually they will be buried in that cemetery where their parents were buried years earlier and where Mrs. Nelson also has a sister and a nephew buried.

Both of the Grays' children, and their families, are members of the eight-hundred-member Trinity Church located in a city a dozen miles to the northwest. For many decades this was a stable county seat that had gradually grown from 2,800 residents in 1920 to nearly 5,000 in 1950. It has always been the largest community in that county. When the interstate highway was constructed, it included two interchanges to service those who had business there. During the next three decades the population nearly tripled as the city grew out to fill in the vacant land near those two interchanges. While scores of rural hospitals were closing, three physicians led the battle to find a new and larger site for what had been a small facility. Today this new and modern hospital draws patients from more than a dozen counties. Several years ago a two-year community college was organized to service a five-county jurisdiction. Today three different chains of supermarkets operate grocery stores in this city. Three motels and four new service stations are located near those interchanges. What once was a weekly newspaper is now published five days a week and the newest addition is a small enclosed shopping mall near the west interchange on the interstate. Twelve years ago the leaders at Trinity Church decided to sell their downtown church building that was constructed in 1921 on a 60-by-150 foot lot and build a new meeting place on a five-acre site out near the interchange. That new shopping mall is less than a thousand feet down that same street. During these twelve years the membership at Trinity has more than doubled to eight hundred, the staff now includes a pastor, a full-time associate minister with major responsibilities for youth ministries, a semi-retired minister of visitation, a half-time children's worker, a half-time director of music, one full-time secretary and a second who works twenty hours a week, a half-time computer operator, and a retired farm couple who serve as custodians. In 1989 the $465,000 budget included over $90,000 for missions and benevolences, and church attendance has increased by nearly 10 percent annually for the past several years. More than one-third of today's members do not live within the municipal boundaries of the city, and several score live more than ten miles away.

Last fall the worship committee decided to increase the number of Christmas Eve services from two to five. As part of that change, the evangelism committee decided they would help publicize it and designed a brochure to be mailed to every household in several zip code areas inviting people to come to one of those five special services.

The committee recruited several retirees to come in one afternoon to sort, count, and package the brochures as part of that bulk mailing effort.

"Hey, wait a minute," exclaimed one of the volunteers. "These say they are to be delivered to every boxholder in Loganville. We can't do that! There's a church of our denomination out there, and they're struggling to stay alive. We don't have any right to raid that congregation! I know some of those people, and they're not going to drive fifteen miles to come here to church on Christmas Eve. This is a waste of money to send them these brochures and it's not right!"

"I happen to know the pastor who serves that congregation," explained a member of the evangelism committee. "He lives in Reedstown and also serves the Loganville church. They always have a Christmas Eve service in the Reedstown church, but they haven't had one at Loganville for years. Reedstown is about nine miles west of Loganville, and we're about fifteen miles to the east. It's easier for people in Loganville to get in their car and drive here on the interstate than to go on those round-about county roads to Reedstown. In fact, I expect we're closer in terms of driving time. Besides that, we do have two families in Loganville who are members here."

"I still don't think it's right for us to be raiding other churches," protested this volunteer. "Here's another package for the post office in La Valle and one for people who get mail out of Hammond. We also have churches of our denomination in those towns. What's going on here? Are we inviting everybody in this county to come here on Christmas Eve?"

"Almost, but not quite," replied the member from the evangelism committee. "We talked about the issue you're raising in our committee two months ago. We'll be running a quarter page ad in the newspaper, and we decided that since that newspaper serves all or parts of five counties, there would be no harm in going beyond the city limits in inviting people. Besides, we are going to have five different and exciting services on Christmas Eve. We decided that most of the recipients of this mailing are adults so they can decide for themselves whether or not they want to come here on Christmas Eve."

"I think I'll go home," declared this volunteer. "My conscience won't allow me to be part of any effort that's going to undercut our sister churches. They need our help, our prayers, and our support. They don't need us to try to steal away their few remaining families!"

A New Context for Living

For many decades Trinity Church was located in and served part of the population of a typical county seat town. In recent years this county seat town has been transformed into what is sometimes referred to as a "sixty-mile city." People come from a thirty- or forty-mile radius, thanks in part to the interstate highway, for a growing array of specialized services. An extreme example of this is that famous shopping mall in West Edmonton, Alberta, that includes under one roof a huge swimming pool, an amusement park, hotel, nearly two dozen theaters, hundreds of retail stores, and scores of other attractions. It attracts visitors from thirty provinces and states.

One a more modest scale the typical sixty-mile city includes a regional hospital, a daily newspaper, at least two travel agencies, several stockbrokers, one or two shopping malls, perhaps a branch of the state university or a community college, a vocational school, several supermarkets, one or two multi-screen theaters, the county courthouse, several gasoline stations, perhaps an independent television station, a state office building, and a variety of other services.

The long-term implications for the church in non-metropolitan America can be understood if we first look at several other changes that have been altering the life-styles of the residents of rural America.

"I was born in a farmhouse five miles out in the country on a winter day in 1932," recalled Ethel Watkins, "but when the Hill-Burton grants made it possible for us to have our own hospital here in town, I went to the hospital to have each of our four children. The fourth was born in 1963 and I was in the hospital for only three days, compared to a week with the first one in 1952."

Today that hospital is one of scores across the country that no longer has an obstetrics unit. The price of malpractice insurance forced it and both of the local physicians to give up the baby business. Today women from that community go to a hospital forty-three miles away to give birth. Most of the patients in this small-town hospital are past fifty years of age.

"I really don't look forward to Nancy driving thirty-five miles each way to go to the university," explained the mother of a high school graduate to her pastor, "but we figure it's cheaper than for her to live in one of the dormitories. It's just three miles from our house to the interstate and less than two miles from where she gets off the interstate to the campus, so it's only a forty-five-minute trip."

"That's interesting," replied the fifty-six-year-old pastor. "My family lived less than forty miles from the college I attended, but at that time no one ever thought of my commuting. It was just assumed that I would live in the dorms. That was part of the fun of going off to college."

"Yes, we wish Nancy could live in the dormitory," sighed the mother, "but it costs so much these days to go to school, that simply is out of the question."

"Yes, that used to be Woolworth's," agreed the grandfather as he walked down the main street in another county seat town of 3,100 residents, "but they closed it several years ago." His thirty-seven-year-old son was back for a visit, and they were showing the twelve-year-old grandson the community where his father had grown up years earlier. "Jerry Nelson bought the building and divided it into four offices," continued the grandfather. "Now we have a veterinarian who specializes in small animals, a stockbroker, a travel agency, and another dentist, but no dime store. The closest thing to a five-and-ten-cent store is a K-Mart about thirty miles east of here."

The church attendance pattern of the Grays, the outreach of Trinity Church into those surrounding small rural communities, that changing pattern of hospital care, the increasing number of students who commute to an institution of higher learning, and the changes on Main Street introduce the new context of doing ministry in non-metropolitan communities. It may be useful to look briefly, however, at a few of other changes before examining the contemporary choices for churches in non-metropolitan America.

One of the changes is the disappearance of the small-town hospital. In 1960 the American Hospital Association reported, 3,973 hospitals with fewer than 100 beds. Today that number is under 2,900 and shrinking. Though a few have grown in size to more than 100 beds, most of that shrinkage represents closings. Another 700 are expected to close by 1996. Most of these 700 will be small, rural, and publicly owned hospitals. Medicare, the increasing specialization in health care, the cost of malpractice insurance, and the shortage of nurses have changed the economic rules for hospital survival.

A second change is that the number of dental school graduates increased from 3,247 in 1960 to 5,585 in 1985, while fluoridated water decreased the number of cavities. One result is the growing number of rural communities that enjoy the services of a resident dentist, but most do without a resident physician. A third change is that increase in accumulated wealth in rural America has attracted a growing number of stockbrokers. A fourth is that a growing number of rural retirees has expanded the opportunities for the small-town travel agency. A fifth change is the expansion of the state university systems of higher education, which has made it easier for an increasing number of students to live at home and commute to school. A sixth is the disappearance of the five-and-ten-cent store from Main Street. A seventh change has been the increasing willingness of residents of rural America to drive fifteen to fifty to seventy-five miles or more for employment, medical care, education, shopping, recreation, special events, entertainment, and other activities.

Behind these and scores of other changes is the completion of President Dwight D. Eisenhower's favorite accomplishment as President of the United States, construction of the interstate highway system. While he was rebuffed by a Democratic-controlled House of Representatives when he first proposed it in early 1955, a year later Congress approved the President's pet project.[1] Completion of this highway network has encouraged a new generation of rural residents to combine the attractiveness of country living with a city paycheck by commuting twenty to thirty or forty miles to work. It has been an influential factor in encouraging employers to locate new sources of employment in what formerly were rural counties. It has been a powerful factor behind the emergence of large regional centers for health care. This highway system also has made it easier for rural residents to commute ten to forty miles for a broad array of services ranging from retail trade to recreation, from medical care to major league baseball, and from education to employment to worship.

The Transformation in Agriculture

Along the rural stretches of that highway has occurred one of the great transformations in the Western world. This was the change in American agriculture from being labor intensive to capital intensive. Money, machinery, and management skills largely replaced the husband, wife, children, hired hand, horses, and mules as the primary resources for successful farming. The pace of this transformation can be illustrated by the fact that farmers such as Walter Gray witnessed all of it in one lifetime.

While the churches have had seventeen or eighteen decades to adjust to the suburbanization of the urban population,[2] this transformation in agricultural America occurred during the lifetime of farmers such as Walter Gray. Therefore it should not be surprising that religious leaders in rural America are still struggling with the consequences of this transformation. The pace of it can be illustrated by a few statistics. The number of tractors on American farms rose from 51,000 in 1917 to a million in 1931 to 1.6 million in 1940 to 4.7 million in 1960. The number of grain combines jumped from 190,000 in 1940 to over a million twenty years later. The number of pickup balers grew from 25,000 in 1941 to 715,000 in twenty years.

The number of people living on farms remained on a plateau of slightly over 30 million through the first four decades of the twentieth century. During the next twenty years it dropped by one-half and by another two-thirds during the next quarter century. In 1957, the first year of that big eight-year postwar exodus from the farm, 2.2 million more people moved off the farm than moved to live on a farm. The previous year that net loss through migration had been only a quarter of a million. The number of African-Americans living on farms plunged from 2.6 million to fewer than a

American Farm Population (Millions)	
1920	31.9
1925	31.2
1930	30.5
1933	32.4
1935	32.2
1940	30.6
1943	26.7
1947	25.8
1950	23.1
1955	19.1
1960	15.6
1965	12.4
1970	9.7
1980*	6.1
1985*	5.4
*New definition	

million during that single decade of the 1960s.

This transformation from labor intensive to capital intensive meant farms had to grow in size in order to support that huge capital investment in machinery. The number of farms in the United States peaked at 6.8 million in 1935 (compared to 4 million in 1880 and 6.5 million in 1920), dropped to 5 million in 1955, plunged to 3 million in 1969, and stood at approximately 2 million in 1989. The average (mean) size of all farms in the United States held steady at approximately 150 acres from 1870 through 1940. By 1952 that figure had climbed to an average of 200 acres per farm and in 1964 it was 332 acres. By 1989 the average farm size had grown to 475 acres. (In looking at these figures on the number of farms and the farm population it should be noted that at least 2 million adults living on farms hold full-time, off-the-farm jobs. It also should be noted that many of the most productive farms are still small and labor intensive. In 1985, for example, San Diego, California, ranked second among the nation's counties in the number of farms and nineteenth in the value of farm products sold, but seven-eights of all farms in San Diego County were under 50 acres in size. It also should be noted that thirteen of the twenty leading counties in the United States in the value of agricultural products sold are in California.)

Average Size of U.S. Farms (in Acres)		
1850	=	180
1870	=	150
1900	=	150
1920	=	140
1930	=	150
1940	=	150
1952	=	200
1964	=	332
1989	=	475

Although space prohibits an exhaustive review of all the factors behind this transformation of life in non-metropolitan America, a few other facts merit mention here. Perhaps the most critical one for the rural churches is the change in the composition of the rural population. The number of people living in rural America has held steady at between 50 and 60 million since 1910. The proportion living on farms, however, has dropped from nearly 60 percent to 10 percent. When Walter Gray was born, well over one-half of all rural Americans lived on farms. Today Walter Gray, his wife, and two of their sons continue as residents of rural America, but none of them live on a farm.

Walter and his wife, Sarah, also symbolize another product of this transformation. They are growing old and have decided to retire in the same county in which they have lived for all their lives. In 1980 seventy-five counties in the United States reported that at least 22.66 percent of the residents had passed their sixty-fifth birthday. To no one's surprise eleven of those counties are in Florida, but twenty-four are in Texas, fifteen in Kansas, six in Missouri, four in Nebraska, and three in Arkansas. If that cutoff point is dropped to include counties in which at least 18 percent of the population are sixty-five or older, Iowa and Kansas rank among the four leading states in the number of retiree counties.

Another statistical indicator that can be used to highlight the localization of the aging population is to compare, on a county-by-county basis, the number of births in a given year with the number of deaths. For the United States as a whole, births outnumber deaths in the typical year by nearly a two-to-one margin. In a couple of hundred counties, however, deaths exceed births in the typical year. As might be expected, because of that large number of sparsely populated rural counties, Texas has more counties in which deaths exceed births than any other state. A close second is Missouri followed by Kansas, Nebraska, Florida (including several urban counties), Arkansas, Oklahoma, Kentucky, Virginia, Iowa, South Dakota, and West Virginia.

Overlapping that aging of the population in hundreds of rural counties has been a change in the economic base. Back in the 1950s, when Walter Gray was still on the farm, agriculture, retail trade, governmental employment (schools, prisons, state, and federal employees stationed in rural areas, county government), the service trades, and manufacturing accounted for most of the personal income of the residents of rural America.[3]

Today the number-one source of personal income in more than five hundred rural counties consists of the checks delivered by the post office. These include Social Security checks, welfare payments, interest and dividends from investments, private pension payments, and checks from governmental pension programs including the military. In 1985 twenty-five counties reported that at least 30.56 percent of all residents were the beneficiaries of Social Security. (The rate for the entire population of the United States in 1985 was 15.15 percent.) Six of those counties were in Florida, six in Michigan, six in Texas, and three in Arkansas. When Walter and Sarah Gray sold their 240-acre farm in 1979 for $2,100 per acre, plus the money they received from the sale of their machinery and livestock, they were able to make after-tax investments that now provide them with a higher net annual income than they ever earned while farming. That small open country church they have belonged to for decades may be short of prospective new members, but it has a solid financial base as long as the Grays are alive.

The Impact of School Consolidation

Other factors should not be overlooked in the context for planning for the church in rural America. For many, the most significant was the consolidation of public school districts. The number of self-governing public school districts in the United States dropped from 127,422 in 1932 to 101,273 in 1946 to 54,773 in 1956 to 23,390 in 1967 to 14,741 in 1987. While the advantages and disadvantages of school consolidation from an educational perspective constitutes one of the most divisive debates of this century, nearly everyone agrees one result was the elimination of one of the most powerful cohesive forces in rural America.

Who Goes to Church?

A second factor, which is more subjective, is that an abundance of survey data suggests that Americans born during the first third of the twentieth century constitute the most churchgoing generation in the nation's history. A combination of denominational loyalties, kinship ties, traditional values, and other influences made this an easy generation for the churches to reach. By contrast, churches must work harder to earn and retain the loyalty of younger generations.

What Is the Future of the Family Farm?

Perhaps the most divisive of all these issues and factors is the future of the family farm. One group of leaders in rural America contend that extraordinary efforts should be made to ensure a future for the family farm. Some contend this will require substantial intervention by the federal government. Others argue that a return to a labor intensive approach to agriculture, a ceiling on land prices, and a reduction in governmental subsidies are critical components of a strategy to preserve the family farm. On the other side are those who are willing to write off the labor intensive family farm of the 1920s as a relic of the past.[4] This emotion-charged and divisive debate makes it difficult to agree on a strategy for the rural church.

Where Are Tomorrow's Preachers?

For dozens of denominational leaders the most subtle and certainly one of the most influential changes is the source of ministers for rural and small-town churches.

Conventional wisdom suggests that for many decades the pastors of rural churches were drawn almost entirely from among those who were born and reared in a farming community. Some went away to school and returned to serve in a subculture they knew because they were a product of rural America. Many others went directly into the parish ministry with little formal academic preparation.

Today the vast majority of seminary students grew up in an urban setting. Many came from a childhood, and perhaps years of adult participation, in a large urban or suburban church. Their world view subsequently was influenced by their experiences in a large state university and in an urban seminary. Many others first accepted Christ through a parachurch organization. When asked to serve the type of rural church Walter and Sarah Gray have spent their lives in, the newly arrived pastor usually encounters some degree of culture shock. They come from a *Gesellschaft* world to serve a *Gemeinschaft* church.

This cultural picture often is complicated by economic factors. In 1906 the average (mean) annual salary of all ministers serving churches outside cities with a population of 25,000 or more was $573. For the General Synod of the Evangelical Lutheran Church in the United States of America that figure was $744. For the Presbyterian Church in the United States the average annual salary for small-town and rural pastors was $977. For the Protestant Episcopal Church the average was $994. For Roman Catholic priests it was $724. For the Methodist Episcopal Church South the average was $681. For rural and small-town Southern Baptist preachers the average cash salary in 1906 was $334. For the Disciples of Christ if was $536.[5] Usually that cash salary was supplemented by free use of a church-owned house. (It is necessary to multiply those salaries by fourteen by provide the equivalent purchasing power of the dollar in 1990.)

Today the compensation package for a recent seminary

graduate, including cash salary, pension, health insurance, car allowance, and a modest stipend for continuing education, often is between $22,000 and $26,000 *plus* housing and utilities. For the congregation averaging 70 at worship, this may average $8 to $10 per worshiper every Sunday.

This picture is further complicated by (a) the fact that many seminary graduates are burdened with $10,000 to $50,000 of debts incurred during those years in school, (b) the Tax Reform Act of 1986 that has designated the only attractive tax shelter available to many middle-income families to be an owner-occupied house, and so the demand is accelerating for housing allowances to replace living in a church-owned dwelling, (c) the annual cost to the church for ministerial pensions is climbing in several denominations, and (d) the annual premiums on health insurance have risen sharply in recent years.

Another way of explaining the current financial squeeze on the small rural church is that in 1989 the average family income for residents of non-metropolitan counties in the United States (in current dollars) was approximately twenty-one times what it had been back in 1906, but the dollar cost for compensating a rural pastor in 1989 was approximately thirty-five to forty times the cost in 1906. This is not to suggest that ministers are overpaid today, but these changes help explain why the leaders in smaller churches feel they are being priced out of the ministerial marketplace. That is precisely what has happened.

Most of today's rural churches were founded back in the days when most people traveled on foot or by horse. The ten- or twenty- or thirty-mile trip "into town" was an all-day, or sometimes an overnight journey. What was designed for one generation may become obsolete with the arrival of new generations.

The construction of the interstate highway system, the expansion of the state system of higher education, the demand for specialized health care services, the increase in leisure time, the separation of the place of residence from the place of employment, that unprecedented drop in the number of Americans living and working all day on farms, the emergence of expensive shopping malls to replace Main Street as a retail center, and the continuing creation of new sources of employment have created the sixty-mile city—usually next to two or three exits from the interstate highway system.

The Generational Gap

The sixty-seven-year-old mother prefers to be treated by her trusted family doctor at the small local hospital while her thirty-two-year-old daughter is willing to drive fifty miles to the clinic that has thirty-seven specialists on the staff. The retired farm couple in their late sixties may continue to buy their groceries at the same store they have patronized for a half century—the one that extended them credit without any questions on several occasions. Their children prefer the once-a-week trip to the big supermarket. The high school that graduated dozens of senior classes during the first half of this century is now a senior citizens' center. After that daily twenty- to sixty-minute ride each way to high school, today's teenagers think nothing of driving into the sixty-mile city for a movie or of commuting to college.

One small-town congregation, founded in 1881, meets in a building constructed in 1903 and is served by a pastor who also serves another congregation. The Sunday morning crowd averages between sixty-five and seventy in attendance and is composed largely of people born before 1940. The younger people, including the adult children of several members, prefer to drive eight or ten or fifteen miles to be part of a worshiping community that averages well over 300 at worship, has two ministers on the staff, a strong youth program, a choir of two dozen regulars plus another dozen who show up to rehearse for those special anthems at Christmas and Easter, a closely graded Sunday school that includes four adult classes, a women's organization with sixty-five active members in five circles, plus a number of other activities and events.

In a typical example of today's sixty-mile city each of the three largest Protestant congregations average well over five hundred at Sunday morning worship. One draws from a thirty-five mile radius and the other two report only a handful of regular attenders who live beyond twenty miles. Each of these three congregations includes more members than ever before in its history. Each has a large program staff and an extensive weekday program. Two of the three broadcast their Sunday morning service over a local radio station. The third video-tapes it, and that edited tape is televised in a half-hour program the following Sunday.

All three of these big churches report that most of the mature members live within the city limits, but close to half of the younger people live beyond the city limits. One of the three has purchased and razed several houses in order to provide the room for a new wing and additional off-street parking. The second of the three, which is not affiliated with any of the old-line Protestant denominations, is less than thirty years old and is growing at the fastest rate, relocated to a larger site several years ago. The third meets in an old building in the central business district near a city-owned parking lot.

What Are the Implications?

From a congregational perspective one of the most visible consequences of the emergence of the sixty-mile city can be seen on Sunday morning. In most of the long-established small-town congregations, the attendance in the typical Protestant congregations includes fewer than a hundred people at worship and most of them were born before 1940.

The younger adults, the bulging nurseries, the big Sunday schools, and the extensive weekday ministries are in the churches in and on the edge of the sixty-mile city. The younger people are willing to travel the longer distance for a broader range of program choices.

Today friendship and kinship ties, the attachment to this sacred place, and denominational loyalties provide a constituency for the small-town congregation, but many of those who are viewed as potential members have decided to make the longer journey to the church that offers a more attractive program.

In addition, among the long-established churches affiliated with one of the old-line Protestant denominations, the churches in the sixty-mile city are more likely to be served by experienced pastors. The pastors with fewer than a dozen years' experience in the parish ministry, including many second-career ministers who come from an urban background, are more likely to be serving in the small rural churches. Many of these congregations also are theologically more conservative than their sister churches from the same denomination located in the sixty-mile city.

Another part of this scenario goes back to the old axiom, "New churches to reach new people." Since most of the old-line denominations (United Methodist, Christian Church [Disciples of Christ], Episcopal Church, Presbyterian Church [U.S.A.], American Baptist Churches, and the United Church of Christ) no longer place a high priority on organizing new congregations, many of the larger and rapidly growing congregations in and near the sixty-mile city are either independent churches or related to one of the younger denominations with an aggressive church-planting strategy. One obvious result is that these tend to be the churches with the large number of young adults, the expanding program, the new buildings, and the large parking lots.

At that branch of the state university system, which originally may have been a state teachers' college, the campus minister is still working on a strategy to serve all those commuter students.

The pastor of the small-town church, who once could

visit four-fifths of his hospitalized parishioners by going to one hospital, now has to travel to three or four widely scattered hospitals to fulfill those pastoral responsibilities.

The ministerial association in the sixty-mile city still meets monthly and has a growing membership, but that membership includes a smaller proportion of the total clergy roster—and at least a dozen of the theologically more conservative or charismatic ministers have organized their own group.

The clientele that supported the small-town grocery store, a new car franchise, variety store, hospital, several physicians, a half-dozen or more churches, the farm implement dealer, a hardware store, and one or two banks is dying off or moving to a retirement center or commuting to the sixty-mile city. The younger generation does not display the same kind of local institutional loyalties. Some will argue that the beginning of this decline in local loyalties can be traced to the closing of the local high school as a part of the public school consolidation strategy of the 1940s or 1950s. Others point to paved roads and better automobiles as the critical factor.

One of the employment centers for residents of many small towns is the new nursing home out on the edge of town. This location can compete with the nursing homes in the sixty-mile city, despite the absence of a nearby hospital, because of lower land and construction costs, a lower wage scale, greater continuity in what is clearly a more dedicated and caring staff, proximity to friends and kinfolk, and the residents' fears of being neglected in a more distant nursing home.

The minister who—after ten to twenty years' experience as a parish pastor in small-town churches—moves to serve a congregation in a sixty-mile city usually encounters considerable cultural discontinuity.

Friendship and kinship ties plus the attachment to that sacred place and denominational allegiance normally are powerful cohesive forces in the small rural congregation. The large church in the sixty-mile city often discovers the personality of the pastor, the ministry of music, the teaching ministry, preaching, and the quality of the program are the influential factors in attracting new members. The larger the congregation, the more relevant Ralph Waldo Emerson's observation, "An institution is the lengthened shadow of one man."

For some pastors, that move also may mean a change from working as the only paid program staff member to being part of a professional program team. For many it means moving from a closely knit community setting that is very supportive of the church to a far more complex setting, which is neutral or even slightly hostile toward the church. One expression of this is the warning to keep the doors locked. Another is the automatic acceptance of the minister as a respected community leader in small-town America, contrasted with the anonymity that goes with being the newest minister in a sixty-mile city.

While some may argue that federal policies affecting the family farm represent the key variable in determining the future of the small rural church, more and more rural residents are commuting to church in cities found at forty-to-one-hundred-mile intervals along the interstate highway system. These emerging urban centers are changing the system of higher education, the delivery of health care services, the shape of retail trade, the style of rural life—and the nature of American Protestantism in the twenty-first century.

What Are the Choices?

For the churches in the sixty-mile city the choices are relatively clear. One is to affirm the new *Gesellschaft* version of contemporary reality and become a large, complex, urban, and heavily programmed congregation that is sensitive and responsive to the religious needs of those younger generations born after 1940. This sensitivity and the resulting ministry may attract people from a twenty-to-thirty-mile radius.

An alternative is to seek to serve those who prefer the *Gemeinschaft* version of reality, specialize in one-to-one relationships, perhaps add a few small groups and be content with smaller numbers.

Another alternative that many nationality parishes and a growing number of theologically conservative congregations have chosen is to recreate a *Gemeinschaft* religious community within that larger *Gesellschaft* urban context. For many families the church becomes their extended family and the only time they leave it is when they go home or go to work.

These smaller congregations outside the sixty-mile city have many options, but the most attractive, to recreate yesterday, rarely is on that list. One of the problems is the economic squeeze resulting from the desire for a full-time resident pastor. One response has been for two or three congregations to share a pastor, but on a long-term basis that usually leads to shrinking numbers in at least one of the churches. Another has been the shared staff of three to ten ministers who serve a larger parish of seven to thirty congregations, but in the long run that has resulted in the closing of many churches. A third has been to "buy time" by securing the part-time services of a retired pastor. A fourth, and one that is increasingly common, is to be served by a part-time pastor who wants time for parenting responsibilities and is married to a spouse with full-time employment. A fifth has been to merge into a church in the sixty-mile city. A sixth is to be served by the minister who is also the part-time director of that new, small nursing home that cannot afford a full-time director. A seventh choice has been to redefine the role and build a larger constituency by attracting new members who live within a ten-to-twenty-mile radius of the meeting place. This usually requires visionary, energetic, creative, productive, and persuasive leadership from an unusually competent and personable pastor.

An eighth alternative, which is chosen by perhaps two

thousand rural churches annually, is to close. A ninth is to attract that retired military chaplain who seeks the combination of a rural life-style and a part-time pastorate. A tenth option, and one which is being advocated by a growing number of regional judicatories, is to encourage small rural congregations to become lay-led religious communities that are not dependent on professional ministerial leadership. Perhaps the fastest growing alternative is to staff them with bivocational ministers who have a full-time secular job.[6] A twelfth alternative is the administrative merger of two churches from different denominational backgrounds that enables people to retain their individual denominational affiliation as part of what is now a federated church.

The option chosen by a growing number of rural churches is to redefine their role by organizing a Christian day school and offering an educational experience based on an explicit Christian value system.[7] This has turned out to be an especially attractive alternative for those churches seeking to reach families with elementary school age children.

Perhaps the most satisfying alternative for many members can be seen in those rural churches located in what have become "retirement communities" in rural sections of Florida, Texas, Wisconsin, Kansas, South Carolina, Iowa, Arkansas, Pennsylvania, New Jersey, Minnesota, Nebraska, California, Arizona, New Mexico, Ohio, Colorado, North Carolina, and Tennessee. In these rural communities the increase in the number of retired adults has enabled long-established churches to double, triple, or quadruple in size. The five critical components of the strategy for attracting retired newcomers appear to be (1) excellent preaching, (2) a strong adult Sunday school, (3) an active and aggressive women's fellowship, (4) attractive weekday programming, and (5) a personable, extroverted, aggressive, creative, persuasive, imaginative, and attractive pastor.[8]

Overlapping that is the growing number of what once were

farming or mining or logging or railroad[9] community churches
that have watched employment in those occupations shrink
and the new economic base become tourism. While this is a
more difficult role, dozens of long-established rural churches
have now redefined their purpose to include ministries with
both short-term visitors and retirees.

The Home Schooling Phenomenon

Perhaps the most distinctive of all the options on this list,
and one available to both small rural churches and to
congregations in the sixty-mile city, is a by-product of
public school consolidation.

Among the factors that have shaped the context for this
option are these: (1) a widely shared conviction that
children often encounter difficulties in learning in a large
and complex setting marked by a high degree of anonymity,
(2) growing dissatisfaction by many parents who are
convinced traditional values are not being taught in public
schools, (3) the increasing proportion of public school
teachers (especially black teachers and administrators) who
choose private schools for their own children, and thus send
a message to parents, (4) the rapidly growing number of
former public school teachers who are choosing home
schooling, (5) the inability of many public schools to satisfy
the demands for greater egalitarianism in the classroom and
still challenge the gifted child, (6) the recognition that few
public schools are prepared to meet the distinctive needs of
developmentally disabled and physically handicapped
children, and (7) parental opposition to busing young
children long distances to school.

This combination of factors plus other considerations has
resulted in an unprecedented increase in the number of
parents who elect to educate their children at home.[10]
During the 1980s nearly every state enacted legislation and
adopted regulations that have eliminated most of the

governmental barriers to home schooling. While detailed statistics are not available, in 1989 at least a half million (double the 1983 total) and perhaps as many as a million American children of elementary school age were being educated at home. Many of the parents choose this option for only a year or two, sometimes as a response to a particular teacher they want their children to avoid.

A common pattern is for the parents to concentrate on academic subjects in the morning and seek socialization opportunities for the children in the afternoon. Thus the small congregation seeking to build a new constituency for tomorrow could consider the possibility of become a center for home schoolers. This could mean drawing people from a twenty-to-thirty-mile radius several times a week including Sunday morning. A church interested in this option will need space to park two dozen motor vehicles, an outdoor playground, a fellowship room with at least 800 square feet of open space, indoor plumbing, two attractive Sunday school classrooms for children and one room for an adult class, a creative pastor or lay volunteer who is knowledgeable about and sympathetic with the home schooling movement and who will take initiative in launching this program, a willingness to become a non-geographical parish, and a supportive stance toward traditional values.

What will be the program? The answer will vary, of course, depending on the adult leadership, but will focus largely on music, teaching pro-social conduct, structured recreation, birthday parties, socialization, encouraging the expression of creative gifts in a group setting, enhancing skills in interpersonal relationships, evening or Saturday parenting classes, the exchange of experiences, Sunday school classes, helping children learn and understand time sequence, teaching moral behavior, enabling both children and parents to meet and make new friends, the sharing of curriculum resources, fellowship, and, in a few states, planning a strategy for relating to the state department of public instruction.

Congregations interested in this option should understand that home schoolers do not constitute a homogeneous group. Perhaps the most publicized segment of that population is composed of conservative Christians who oppose the secularization of the public schools. A second and radically different group is drawn from those who identify with the New Age world view. They oppose the public schools because the public schools do not nurture New Age values such as reincarnation, oneness with nature, the law of Karma, and ecology. A third, and perhaps the largest group, is composed of well-educated parents who espouse a "liberal" viewpoint on ecology, conservation, and politics, but display great skepticism about the effectiveness of any large bureaucratic institution. A fourth and growing group is composed of parents of developmentally disabled or physically handicapped children who are convinced the public schools will not enable their children to realize their full God-given potential. The point of commonality is that all are willing to make substantial personal sacrifices on behalf of their children. Perhaps no one congregation can reach and serve more than one or two of these four groups of home schoolers.

Overlapping two or three of these choices is an option that more than a few of those long-established small rural churches located on a sparsely traveled rural road have dared to choose. That alternative is relocation and was discussed in chapter 5. These congregations have relocated to a highly visible, easily accessible, and larger parcel of land a few miles away along a major highway, constructed a new meeting place to house a more extensive program, and launched an aggressive evangelistic effort to attract their new neighbors. Again the success stories among these ventures usually reflect the crucial importance of competent, creative, aggressive, persuasive, and visionary pastoral leadership. This, of course, also is a compatible choice for a congregation that decides to create a new constituency from one or two of those home schooling groups or to open a Christian day school.

Finally, a word needs to be said to legitimatize the choice picked by tens of thousands of small rural churches. This is to specialize in ministry largely with mature adults. Many congregations find it impossible to affirm this choice. They are convinced "our future depends on our being able to attract young people." In hundreds of rural counties in Kansas, Pennsylvania, North Carolina, Texas, Florida, New Jersey, Illinois, and other states that is a misreading of reality. The economy is designed to attract and retain mature adults, not to provide satisfying and well-paid jobs for younger people. The absence of a modern telephone system that can service employers relying on telecommunications is only one of several barriers to that widely shared dream of "keeping our young people here in this community." The aging of the rural population makes a ministry with mature adults a choice that deserves not only serious consideration, but strong affirmation.[11]

Two of the most urgent questions before many of the churches in the sixty-mile cities and in rural America are: (1) who will choose the course of action we should seek to implement and (2) what are the criteria that will be used in making that choice? Who will do that in your church?

Notes

1. For an account of Eisenhower's interest in the interstate highway system, see Stephen S. Ambrose, *Eisenhower: The President* (New York: Simon & Schuster, 1984), pp. 251, 547-49.
2. Two excellent books on the suburbanization of the population are Kenneth T. Jackson, *Crabgrass Frontier* (New York: Oxford University Press, 1985) and John D. Stelgoe, *Borderland* (New Haven: Yale University Press, 1988).
3. An introduction to the changing economic base of rural America is Lloyd D. Bender et al., *The Diverse Social and Economic Structure of Nonmetropolitan America* (Washington: Economic Research Service of the United States Department of Agriculture Rural Development

Research Project No. 49, September 1985). A popular account is "What's Happening to Our Town," *Newsweek,* August 15, 1988, pp. 28-29. The impact of the arrival of the retirees is discussed in Bill Richards, "Old Money: Influx of Retirees Pumps New Vitality into Rural Towns, Creating Both Jobs and Tension," *The Wall Street Journal,* August 5, 1988, and Ross K. Baker, "Six Trix Pix Slix," *American Demographics,* January 1989, page 80. An ideological analysis is offered by Barbara Hargrove, "The Future of Rural Populism," *Society,* January/February 1989, pp. 39-44.

4. Two radically different perspectives on what would be needed to preserve the family farm can be found in Marty Strange, *Family Farming* (Lincoln: University of Nebraska Press, 1988) and Clifton B. Luttrell, *The High Cost of Farm Welfare* (Washington, D.C.: Cato Institute, 1989), One illustration of the divisive nature of this debate concerns the price of farmland. Should public policy be designed to keep the price of farmland low in order to make it more economically attractive for young adults to go into farming? Or should land prices be allowed or encouraged to rise in order to encourage marginal farmers and older farmers to sell, thus creating opportunities for a younger generation to move to the farm? See also Elmer W. Learn et al., "American Farm Subsidies: A Bumper Crop," *The Public Interest,* Summer 1986, pp. 66-78; Jim Schwab, *Raising Less Corn and More Hell* (Urbana: University of Illinois Press, 1988); Theodore R. Lyman, *New Seeds for Nebraska* (Menlo Park, Ca.: SRI International, 1988); and Truman Brown, "Shaping the Future of the Urban-Fringe Church," *Church Administration,* May 1988, pp. 6-8. A provocative essay on the struggle for survival in the small-town school is Bob Cole, "Teaching in a Time-Machine: The 'Make-Do' Mentality in Small-Town Schools," *Phi Delta Kappa,* October 1988, pp. 139-44.

5. United States Bureau of the Census, *Religious Bodies, 1906* (Washington, D.C.: Government Printing Office, 1910), Part I, pp. 93-98.

6. John Y. Elliot, *Our Pastor Has an Outside Job* (Valley Forge, Pa.: Judson Press, 1980) and Luther M. Dorr, *The Bivocational Pastor* (Nashville: Broadman Press, 1988).

7. For a less than fully sympathetic, but exceptionally thorough analysis of the fundamentalist Christian school, see Alan Peshkin, *God's Choice* (Chicago: The University of Chicago Press, 1986). This scholarly study also includes an excellent bibliography. It should be noted, however, that the majority of church-operated elementary schools do not resemble the school described by Peshkin.

8. Lyle E. Schaller, *Expanding Ministries with Retirees, Seasonal Visitors and Tourists* (New York: United Church for Homeland Ministries, 1987); Lyle E. Schaller, "Is the Pastoral Ministry a Personality Cult?" *The Clergy Journal,* February 1987, pp. 34-35. For a fascinating account of retirement centers as a contemporary expression of community, see Frances Fitzgerald, *Cities on a Hill*

(New York: Simon & Schuster, 1986), pp. 20-21, 203-45, 390, 414. A wealth of statistical data can be found in Charles F. Longino, Jr., *State to State Migration Patterns of Older Americans for Two Decades* (Coral Gables, Fla.: Center for Social Research in Aging, 1986) and Charles F. Longino, Jr., and Steven G. Ulmann, *The Economically-Advantaged Retiree* (Coral Gables, Fla.: Center for Social Research in Aging, 1988).

9. A classic account of the impact of technological change in a rural railroad community is W. F. Cottrell, "Death by Dieselization: A Case Study in the Reaction to Technological Change," *American Sociological Review,* June 1951, pp. 358-65.

10. The research on the growth of home schooling is still in the early stages, but among the respected researchers studying this subject are Patricia M. Lines, Stuart Wright, Maralee Mayberry, James W. Tobak, Perry A. Zirkel, Mary Anne Pittman, N. J. Linden, John Holt, Sue S. Greene, E. Alice Law Beshoner, and Stephen Arons.

11. See Frank Hutchison, "Coming to Grips with an Aging Church," *The Christian Century,* February 22, 1989, pp. 206-8, for an affirmation of this role.